MANIFESTING WITH ALIGNMENT

7 Hidden Principles to Master
the Energy of Thoughts and Emotions

How to Raise Your Vibration Instantly
and Shift to the Frequency of Your Desires

RYUU SHINOHARA

Omen
Publishing

The Manifestor Masterlist
(It'll be near impossible without this...)

This Masterlist includes:

✓   Top 3 daily habits to maximize your manifesting abilities.

✓   Simple layout to track your progress.

✓   Instructions to help you get started today!

The last thing I want is for you to read this book and forget everything you read...

Let's make manifestation a daily habit!

>> Scan the QR Code above with your smartphone
to receive your free Manifestor Masterlist <<

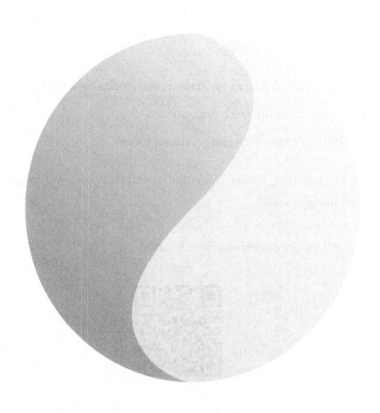

Table of Contents

CHAPTER SIX

CHAPTER SEVEN

INTRODUCTION

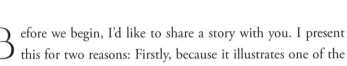

Before we begin, I'd like to share a story with you. I present this for two reasons: Firstly, because it illustrates one of the biggest problems associated with approaching manifestation, and secondly, because it was an avoidable tragedy that touched me deeply. So, let's reflect upon someone who was once a close friend of mine.

My friend—I'll call her Eve—worked in a highly competitive sales organization that consumed nearly every aspect of her life. She had read many sales-related and so-called "metaphysical" books that taught salespeople how to make their financial dreams come true. She had even posted a picture of a brand-new sports car on the wall in her office. Eve believed that if she spent enough time focusing on that photo (along with doing her other manifestation practices), that she would be successful enough in sales to buy that car. Unfortunately, she never got the chance to purchase or drive it. She passed away from a heart attack in her mid-thirties.

You see, sales had been an all-consuming part of Eve's adult life. She had always felt called to the profession. However, the dedication and commitment needed for the work had an unpleasant side effect: *stress.*

The day-to-day pressures and the constant strain resulting from being flanked by corporate demands on one side and client satisfaction on the other can take its toll. As a sales representative, it can be easy to attach your feelings and moods to the actions of your clients. One day, you're ecstatic over a large sale, the next day you're deflated over that big deal that fell through.

Once Eve had accepted the stressful ups and downs as 'part of the game,' she began to forge emotional reactions that even she was unaware of. When met with failure, on the surface she had learned to say things like, "Oh well, that's how things work, I guess." But deep in her subconscious mind, she felt the same as when she'd brought a grade school report card home with a low mark on it—she was still battling feelings of shame and failure. Of course, when Eve was successful, she was 'doing great' and felt 'on top of the world.' This up-and-down rollercoaster of thoughts and emotions made her react, like Pavlov's dog, to any stimuli attached to outside events, resulting in her being happy or sad; confident or deflated. It never occurred to Eve that her journey toward manifestation was tied to this mental and emotional rollercoaster. Needless to say, her lack of success at manifesting what she wanted became just another series of failures for her. This was especially true when anyone reminded her that her new approach to success had met an apparent setback. Eventually, in Eve's case, her body could no longer handle the stress, and sadly, Eve never got to drive that brand-new sports car.

Eve's tragedy provides us with a lesson in how many people attempting to use the Law of Attraction can meet with frustration and failure. Why does this happen? I think it is because there is an element of the law that is commonly ignored. In this book, I'll show you exactly what that is and how using it can prepare you for a life of more ease, flow, and effortless manifestation. Let's get started!

THE 'SECRET'
MOST PEOPLE ARE MISSING

Whether you've been studying the Laws of Manifestation for a while or not, you've no doubt encountered famous individuals who have promoted these laws and told stories of how they work in their lives. But there is something you may not have realized: What they are relating has to do with the positive tangible results of their practices. It's a rare thing to hear a famous person speak about how they managed their emotions or controlled their thoughts in the face of contrast and adversity. True, they may tell you about the negative experiences they've overcome, but do they talk about how to deal with day-to-day mental or emotional turmoil?

You may have been reading about the Laws of Manifestation— and you may have started putting that good advice into action. But … try as you might, nothing happens. Things stay the same; physical abundance doesn't manifest. What are you doing wrong? After all, some of the most trusted names in the media have sworn that these laws work. Well, I'm going to let you in on a secret…

You weren't being lied to. The Laws of Manifestation and Attraction DO work. But many of the teachers and students who talk about these laws leave out some crucial information. You see, those who have had so much success with manifesting had to first overcome certain hurdles (invisible to the eye), and that resolve and commitment eventually cleared the way for manifestations to occur. The attributes that helped them get to where they are, dwell within the mental and emotional levels of all of our beings. In order to manifest your desired reality, you need to master your thoughts and feelings. This is the basis of what I'm going to teach you in this book.

Within these chapters, you'll encounter Seven Hidden Principles that will help you along the path that leads to becoming a master of the energy responsible for manifestation. This is accomplished by bringing awareness to how we allow our outer environment to affect our inner state and subsequent manifestations. People and situations that negatively (or positively) affect our thoughts and emotions can create serious hurdles, and we need to clear those hurdles before we can resonate with a desired reality. Matching your internal state with the external reality you want to attract is what facilitates manifestation—this is how you draw what you truly desire to yourself on a moment-by-moment basis.

By following this path, you will discover methods of how to choose your thoughts and emotions consciously to create a new internal paradigm of beliefs. This new paradigm will replace your pre-conditioned reactions to problems and situations in your life. For most of us, the way we respond to situations in our lives actually prevents us from getting what we want. We resonate energetically with what we don't want rather than what we do want. We have to shift our state and attitudes—and when we do, we jump into the driver's seat of our destiny. Nothing 'out there' will ever significantly alter your inner response to reality, and thus your ability to manifest what you want. That is entirely up to *you*.

MY INNER JOURNEY

When I first discovered the Law of Attraction, like many other people who come across this type of esoteric information, I was in it for external gains. I wasn't worried about my inner reality—what mattered most to me was what I was able to see, hear, smell, taste, and touch. I was unaware of my 'sixth sense,' if you will. Even though I knew I had to "believe it to see it," the components of my beliefs (thoughts and emotions) were secondary to what I was experiencing physically. For me, taking action to get things was more important than reflecting on who I was being. Reacting was more important than responding. What I was witnessing externally was more 'real' to me than what I was experiencing internally.

Until that point in my life, my behaviors, intentions, and choices had become a habit. They were automatic; ingrained into the subconscious layers of my mind and body. And, since we know that thoughts and emotions create our reality, it is safe to say that at the time, I was creating my reality unconsciously. I used to believe that life happened to me, not through me. In other words, I did not believe I was the creator of my reality. Life was trying to teach me lessons, but I thought of them as punishments or obstacles.

Eventually, this up-and-down cycle of trying to change my reality unconsciously led me to dive deep into my research—I was sure I'd find the answer in one of the hundreds of books on the subject. The deeper I went, the more I understood and believed that the only thing I should be prioritizing was my inner state of being. Slowly but surely, my outer reality became less and less relevant. Although I was still experiencing the events in the mundane world, I was no longer identifying with my day-to-day experiences. I became flexible in how I viewed the world, and learned to adapt readily to anything that brought a sense of negativity into my awareness. I accepted that "what is, is," and reminded myself in every situation that I had a choice—I could choose to feel good, light, and uplifted, or I could allow situations to trigger fear, frustration, or anger. The feel-good decisions were always the right ones.

UNCONDITIONAL LIVING

Feeling good, independent of the conditions you find yourself in, is the ultimate state for anyone who wants to make major breakthroughs in their life. To live without judging negatively or reacting unconsciously to the conditions in your life—in other words, to live 'unconditionally'—is to live as a conscious creator of your reality. This isn't to say that you shouldn't desire to have nice things in your life. The Bhagavad Gita, the sixth poem in the great Hindu epic "Mahabharata" says this:

> *"Detachment is not that you own nothing.*
> *Detachment is that nothing owns you."*
> **- Vyasa (from the Bhagavad Gita)**

When you allow yourself to feel good, you will find it easier to shift into your desired frequency, and you'll begin to attract the things you truly want in life. By living unconditionally, and detaching from outcomes, conditions will arise in your life as a natural side effect.

When we're able to gauge our state of being, we can figure out what brings us joy, fulfillment, and happiness—and how to adopt the perspectives to draw those things to us. The question is: "What do you truly want?" There is no point in tuning into frequencies that attract things to you but do not fulfill you. For example, many people want to be a celebrity because they think they want fame, fortune, and attention, but when they receive it, they realize it's not what they truly want. Within this book, we'll be covering how to bring clarity to what it is your soul truly desires.

Manifestation is a product of both the mind and body; our thoughts and emotions play a huge role in our ability to manifest the direction of our lives and all the things in it.

By reading this book, you will come to understand the role your thoughts and emotions play in your day-to-day life, and how this affects what you attract. This understanding helped me to overcome my challenges, and continues to assist me in dealing with stressful situations. Once freed from the ups and downs of conditional living, I began to live in the realm of infinite possibility—a place where we can recognize the greatest potential of every moment, whether it's considered bad or good from an outsider's perspective. It's a simple premise, but it works—as you'll soon find out!

CHAPTER ONE

The Foundation of Energy – Uncovering the Essence of Mind and Body

When considering the Laws of Manifestation, it's easy to assume that your primary focus should be the physical items you seek to acquire. This is a key error. Why? Because if we want to manifest the life we truly want to live, we need to prepare ourselves internally first. Physical reality is like a mirror. It is the mere reflection of our internal world. If, internally, we feel abundant in health, wealth, and love, this feeling will manifest externally. Everything starts within. This brings us to the first of our Seven Hidden Principles ...

PRINCIPLE #1:
Prioritize Your Inner Reality.

What Is Alignment? Understanding alignment is simple. In essence, alignment is our natural state of being. Happiness and peace make up the essence of who we are. Expressing love, joy, and excitement is what we are designed to do. When our mind, body, and soul are in perfect harmony, these states of being permeate our physical and spiritual selves.

The only time, however, that we experience alignment, is when we are not resisting situations we encounter in our physical reality. When we are 'in alignment,' we are moving through life effortlessly, knowing that everything that harmonizes with our desires is ready to present itself—all we have to do is let it in! Rather than forcing circumstances to get what we want, we shift our state and awareness to align with what is already there. Manifesting with ease does not come from the effort of the ego-self … it comes from the soul. Therefore, what you truly want is already in tune with who you are. In order to shift into this soul alignment, there can be no internal blocks—the mind, heart, and spirit need to be on the same page.

YOUR INSTRUMENT OF CREATION

Each of us possesses an immensely powerful instrument of creation. When it's misused, that instrument can cause us a lot of suffering and struggle. On the other hand, if we master this instrument, we can tune into the frequency of everything we could ever ask for. This instrument is called the 'mind and body,' and it's composed of two parts: thoughts which spin from the mind, and emotions which emanate from the physical body. This is a tool that is meant to work *for* you—not the other way around.

Working with our instrument of creation is not as easy as it sounds. You see, when we look at our surroundings, it is easy to assume that what we see is reality. Our reactions to our immediate environment are related to preconceived ideas about that so-called reality. For example, if something doesn't go the way we want it to, we react with frustration, anger, or sadness. Why? Because those emotional reactions are stored in a subconscious repository—and when X situation occurs, we dig into that storage cupboard and respond with Y. Over time, we end up with a huge collection of conditioned reactions to just about any situation we could ever encounter. Sure, the details change from time to time and the settings change—but it's always the same old story: X situation equals Y reaction.

The one true constant is that we use 'like frequencies' to match 'like vibrations,' and we end up manifesting the same things and the same circumstances again and again: the same old things we don't want, in different "clothing."

In this book, I will show you how to master your mind-body instrument to manifest what you choose rather than manifesting randomly. Your manifestations will no longer be haphazard consequences of your pre-conditioned beliefs and perspectives. We will cover how to control whatever is keeping you from manifesting your best life, so that you no longer manifest situations in your life that have little to no bearing on what your soul desires. You will learn how to select a timeline in which circumstances work for you and your fulfilment.

OUR VIBRATIONAL REALITY

When we think of the Universe as a solid mass of matter, we are subscribing to an illusion. The truth is that we exist in a vibrational Universe. Our vibrational generator creates everything we experience in our lives, and right now, your generator is probably filled to the brim with pre-conditioned ideas and energetic reactions for every situation you encounter. That vibrational energy reaches out and attracts things into your life—it is natural, direct, and flawless.

At any given moment, we are attracting things to us that are in vibrational resonance with the frequency at which our vibrations emanate. In a bad mood? You are attracting energy that vibrates in tandem with your mood, and if you're there long enough, you'll manifest a hot mess. Happy? Same thing … appreciation and gratitude for what is and what could be will always be rewarded by the Universe.

How does this work? Consider, for example, that a friend wants to spend quality time with her dad, who's an avid bird photographer. Her dad uses a small tool called a 'duck call' that, when our friend blows into it, creates the sound of a duck's vocalization. This can be compared to our pre-conditioed beliefs. When our friend blows into the duck call, the sound that comes out is vibrating at a frequency that draws ducks toward her and her dad—and he captures stunning close-up photos. In other words, the frequency of the sound vibration harmonizes with real ducks, and ducks are attracted to the area. The sound does not attract eagles, parrots, or pigeons because its frequency does not resonate with those birds. It only attracts ducks. In the same manner, the vibrational signature of our energy attracts items and circumstances that exist in harmony with that same energy.

All of this begins with thought. How? Well, our brains produce electrical energy, which creates vibrations that express themselves through our imagination. This in turn activates another component of manifesting: our emotions, which are responsible for generating a magnetic field around us. As noted earlier, everything in the Universe is vibrational in nature. Therefore, the electrical energy of our thoughts and magnetic energy of our emotions attract like vibrations (in a similar manner to the duck call attracting ducks). *Like attracts like.*

Everything that exists in the cosmos has a unique vibrational signature. For example, a radio station will always be sending out an electrical signal (similar to our thoughts), but what determines the music that plays on our radio is the frequency of that signal (similar to our emotions). If you want to tune into a particular radio station, you have to first, have good signal going out to hear the music clearly, and second, tune your radio to the same frequency at which that station broadcasts. In a similar manner, you are the radio, and you need to send a clear signal and tune yourself to the frequency of the things or experiences you wish to manifest.

We manifest continuously, attracting to ourselves each moment of our current reality. When we understand that manifestation is always in effect, this elevates the power of Principle #1. We begin to notice and witness the relationship between our thoughts and emotions (our inner reality), and what we are experiencing physically.

UNDERSTANDING OUR STATE OF BEING

When we delve into the subject of our "mind, body, and spirit," we need to understand what these words mean and why they are important. In this subchapter, I explain what our state of being is and how it relates to our vibrational frequency.

Our state of being is composed of three layers: the Conscious Mind, the Subconscious Mind, and the Unconscious Mind.

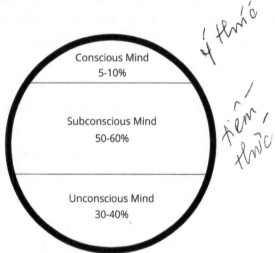

Conscious Mind
5-10%

Subconscious Mind
50-60%

Unconscious Mind
30-40%

- **The Conscious Mind:**

  This is the layer of the mind at which you are neither distracted by your outer reality (people, places, things, events, etc.), nor by your inner reality (thoughts, feelings, fears, etc.). Your attention is centered, and you are aware of what is. When we find ourselves in this place, we are conscious of the choices and decisions we make. It is also within this layer of the mind that we are more aware and present with certain aspects of our being—like how we are thinking and feeling. Changes in your state of being start here.

• The Subconscious Mind:

Your subconscious represents your personality and your attitude. This is the layer where patterns are formed; it is composed of the thoughts you think often and the emotions you feel repeatedly. Some beliefs and conditioning can reside within this layer.

• The Unconscious Mind:

This layer is hidden from your awareness. (Think, for example, of how your digestive system and immune system operate without you doing anything.) When your thoughts and emotions become ingrained habits, they are stored in this layer—and it is in this layer that your deepest and more stubborn belief systems and conditioning reside.

Now, in order to begin changing our state of being, we need to begin clearing out every layer, top to bottom. Think of it as a three-story house that needs some tidying up. We begin cleaning on the top floor (the conscious mind), work down to the middle floor (the subconscious mind), and finally to the bottom floor (the unconscious mind). Ideally, we want to live our lives from the conscious and subconscious layers, because to be unconscious is to be at the mercy of our habits and conditioning. However, we can't avoid filling up this unconscious layer; it will always have some say in how we are thinking and feeling. All we can do is work diligently, cleaning out the floors regularly so that we can have the unconscious layer work in our favor (at most, for achieving short term goals or maintaining small, positive habits).

Within our minds, there resides a voice. Whether this voice works in our favor or not is completely dependent on how conscious we are of it. It's the part of our mind that we can refer to as our "internal dialogue," and it's composed of the mental chatter that floods our brains on a moment-by-moment basis. To show you how prevalent this chatter is, try this: Stop the thoughts that are running through your mind, completely, just for a minute. Do that now.

Unless you happen to be an experienced meditator, I'm sure you were unable to keep your thoughts at bay for even a few seconds. Why is this? It's simple: We are receiving information from our internal and external environment constantly, and we use our internal dialogue constantly to "make sense" of our inner world and surroundings. For example, our internal dialogue tells us that a chair is a chair. But it also tells us how we should feel about that chair. It is, in effect, a channel for all the decisions we make, as well as for the conditioned thoughts and emotions that reside in our subconscious and unconscious layers. Consider the following formulas to outline and improve your understanding of these concepts (• represents 'multiplied by' and 'X' represents the number of repetitions): Memory = Thought + Emotion Attitude = (Thought + Emotion) • X Beliefs = Attitudes • X State of Being = Beliefs • X

Eventually, our collection of memorized and repeated thoughts and emotions are stored in our subconscious mind, and as a result, constitutes our state of being. Every time we store new information in our subconscious mind, there is a natural tendency for us to focus more on things that confirm and support it. Think about when you buy a new car, and suddenly, it seems as though everyone in your neighborhood has the same car. This is how our minds work. The more confirmations we find to back up and support our beliefs, the more we believe them. It eventually gets to the point where we go from *believing* something to be true to *knowing* it to be true.

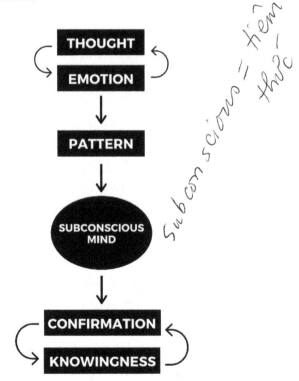

Our internal dialogue is often a direct reflection of who we are being at any given moment. However, the more conscious we are of our internal dialog, the less power it has over us. The elements of our current state of being are a result of us either unconsciously allowing ourselves to be conditioned or choosing consciously which states of being we want to live by.

When your conditioning runs your state of being, your experiences don't always reflect your hoped-for reality. For example, if a woman was to grow up in an abusive household, this conditioning would carry over to her adulthood. As a result, feelings of unworthiness and a victim mentality could pervade her life. If not dealt with, this state of being will lead to thoughts, actions, and reactions that reflect it, and in the end, this person's external reality will begin to reflect that which is being internally reaffirmed constantly.

Now, let's take a look at this from a different angle. Another example might be an anxious person who, even though he might have built great wealth and financial abundance, still feels deep down that 'there will never be enough.' He tuned into the right frequency to manifest material wealth but operates from a lower level of vibration, one that doesn't resonate with his authentic-self. Alternatively, another person might live in poverty, but is content and happy with where and who they are. They operate at a higher level of vibration but have not tuned into a frequency of material wealth.

Thus, the goal is not *only* to change your frequency or *only* to raise your vibration. It's to do both. It's to attract what you want externally, while also having a sense of fulfillment and wholeness within. We do this by memorizing what it feels like when we operate at a higher vibration (joy, peace, excitement, etc.), and then using that feeling to tap into the right frequency (health, wealth, love, etc.), thus attracting what we truly desire.

To get this right the first time, you want to be extremely clear on the direction you want to go and how you want to *be* in a general sense. Understanding yourself and what makes the fire within you light up is essential, as you'll find out in a later chapter. When it comes to manifesting, if you want to alter your current reality, you must take the steps necessary to shift into an entirely new state of being.

So, all of this sounds great, right? But how do we do it? We tend to live in what can be called a bubble of perception. Imagine for a moment that you are sitting inside a big plastic bubble. Whenever you look out, you see only a reflection of yourself. It's quite a dull existence living inside this bubble, and even though you have the power to attract any items or circumstances you desire, you are sending out limited vibrational signals. Even more importantly, the vibrational signals you're sending out match the images inside your bubble—so you are only attracting things that reflect your old, conditioned thoughts and emotions.

I'm using this example because I want you to understand an important point about manifestation. For you to begin to change the reality you are experiencing, first you must be aware of the reality you are creating right now. When something happens in your life, no matter how small or seemingly insignificant it might be, reflect on it and be mindful that a past 'state of being' generated it. When you do this, you realize how, when, and where the seed of your current situation germinated. Even if you can't pinpoint exactly what caused any given event, just be aware that there is a reason for everything that occurs in your life—always. Seeking to know the reason is not meant as a punishment, nor is knowing the reason meant to diminish you in any way. We endeavor to discover the cause of such events so that we can use them for growth and expansion, and as reminders for us that we need to tune into and choose what we want to experience. As you get used to doing this, it will become easier to consistently alter your thoughts and emotions so that you can change what you receive and create in your life.

> *"Until you make the unconscious conscious,*
> *it will direct your life and you will call it fate."*
> **- Carl Jung**

When your circumstances are no longer generated by your past unconscious self, but instead are based on your new conscious and high-vibrational self, magical things begin to happen in your life. Not only will it feel great to be in this new state, but you'll become a magnet for exactly the types of circumstances and conditions you want to attract. This is what it means to overcome your limitations and manifest with alignment.

Later on, I'll show you how to overcome your limitations. After all, who wants to see the same movie playing over and over again? Especially the ones you're tired of watching!

THE REASON BEHIND HUMAN SUFFERING

Why do human beings suffer? There are many reasons, but if you break it down to fundamentals, it is always the same. The cause of our suffering is directly related to our ideas of lack. While we can point to many other things: trauma, poor health, bad finances, or negative relationships, it's our concept of lack that drives our suffering.

There are many obvious situations that cause us to suffer. Sadness over the death of a loved one. Extended illness. Difficulties related to our job. Loneliness. All these situations can leave us feeling current or impending lack. Why do I mention this? Because a sense of lack—be it a lack of love, health, peace, companionship, etc.—can affect a person's ability to manifest their desires.

If you wish to master manifestation, you need to understand that the Universe, by its nature, is ever expanding and infinitely abundant. Lack does not exist in the Universe; lack is illusory. Consider, for example, the following scene: It's a gorgeous, warm summer's day. You are immersed in a cool stream in a forest, lying on your back, a canopy of green trees above you. You can do one of three things in this stream: You can be grateful for this beautiful day and relax so you can flow with the stream's current. You can delight in swimming with the current and travel downstream quickly, with little effort. Or, you can swim against the current. Which choice do you think will cause suffering? Swimming against the current, of course! If you 'go with the flow of your inner nature,' everything will unfold with ease. But if you swim against the current, you push against the flow.

Similarly, if you focus on lack—thinking about what you *don't* have, rather than being grateful for what you *do* have—you are pushing against the nature of the Universe. Rather than regretting that we lack something we want, we must celebrate the abundance of what we do have—that is the way to move in tandem with the Universe. Feeling good is the path to surrendering to and receiving the Universe's abundance.

When we have a negative perspective about something, however, we are resisting; we are acknowledging that something is missing. Resistance happens when we are moving against the flow of the Universe. If you are focusing on abundance, on the other hand, you are in tune vibrationally and you feel good. Simple, right? Well, it's just as simple to allow lack and suffering to take over. Many people's stories of suffering are created based on their sense of lack and limitation—because they concentrate on what once was but is now lost, or what never was but others have—instead of concentrating on the positive potential of every moment they experience and what could be.

There are, of course, countless reasons that suffering exists in the world. However, if you follow the path of circumstances that has led to a single individual's suffering, chances are you will find it rooted in their imaginary concept of lack. Lack of wealth. Lack of power. Lack of love. These illusions—all related to fear—trickle down as actions with negative outcomes.

So, what can we do to free ourselves from the misconception of lack? Since your thoughts and emotions create your reality, you can counteract the illusion of lack by doing the following: Rather than focusing on what you don't have, focus on what you do have, and all that you are receiving and will receive. Any time you receive something, such as money or a gift, make a point of focusing on it and validating it. Even if it's a single dollar, you can acknowledge it by saying: "See, I am being given more abundance!" At the same time, embrace the positive emotions that show up—celebration is another form of showing gratitude. When we show gratitude for what we have, we tune into the frequency of having.

> *"Gratitude is the ultimate state of receivership."*
> **- Dr. Joe Dispenza**

At first, celebrating small signs of abundance might seem strange, especially if you have big dreams and ambitions. But the truth is, if you make this a consistent practice, you build a new default program within your subconscious mind. Your natural inclination will always be to move towards, focus on, and see abundance, in everything you experience. Energy flows where attention goes. So, the more you give your attention to the abundance you do have in your life, the more of it will show up. Throughout this book, we will be covering exactly *how* to optimize your attention, so it is always focused on abundance. This new way of living will develop a new frequency, and sooner than you think, the Universe will begin to match you with new circumstances—and not just another dollar!

CHAPTER TWO

Internal Blueprint – Recognition of the Conditioned and Authentic-self

O ne of the most difficult parts of manifesting is letting go of the perceptions we have developed throughout our lives. This is an exceptionally important point to understand. Too often, when we discover a better way to conduct our lives, we commit to going all in and pledge to do whatever is necessary to make changes. But when something unexpected occurs, we discover that a formidable 'guard,' designed to protect our old beliefs is standing in our way. These beliefs have been handed down to us from the time we first learned how to communicate: our parents, relatives, friends, and acquaintances have told us what to say, think, and believe.

Not only that, every day of our lives we encounter programming in the form of media, government, corporate bosses, and other authority figures. Over time, our 'guard' incorporates these ideas into our inner belief system, and uses those beliefs to influence how we think, feel, and react to each situation we encounter.

In this chapter, we will discover how to recognize the guard for what it really is. I will show you how your guard is really your jailor and that it is no more your friend than iron bars are in a prison. We will cover some new perspectives and simple methods you can use when it comes to freeing yourself from the energetic jail that has been holding you back from manifesting your true desires.

Now, let's take a closer look at what I mean. Let's begin by introducing the main principle of this chapter....

PRINCIPLE #2:
Shift Your Meaning, Shift Your Feeling.

THE EGO-SELF

It's been said that the older you get, the more attached you become to familiar things. For example, have you ever been with an older person who insists on eating the same things when they go out to a restaurant? Perhaps their home resembles a museum—filled with artifacts from their past. Or maybe they love an old garment so much they wear it until the fabric falls apart.

There are many reasons that so many older people fall into this attachment trap—nostalgia, lack of motivation, and security top the list. It is common for people, as they move into their golden years, to feel vulnerable to dangers lurking in their environment. This concern is instinctual—and it's rooted in our early ancestors' development and need for survival.

As we age, life seems to pose more risks for us, and to protect ourselves, we tend to avoid change and cling to the familiar. We assume that the identity we've built has to defend itself from everybody and everything that challenges it. This is merely an extension of the survival instinct that has allowed our species to exist and evolve when we were faced with dangerous predators and circumstances. While this instinct was useful when we lived in caves in the wild jungle and needed to avoid large predators, nowadays it's not so helpful. It makes it difficult to accept change, even when change is beneficial. In most of today's world, we no longer need to fear threats of wild animals, rival tribes, or natural disasters, so this survival mechanism is, by and large, no longer completely necessary. Although it's still useful for the rare situations in which we find ourselves in physical danger, now we use this built-in mechanism primarily to keep us safe in our mental and emotional realities. For example, we build our ego-self-identity over time, and it helps us survive and thrive in the modern world. It helps us sustain our social status relative to the environment we grew up in; it allows us to move through the world with a persona that helps us accommodate, navigate, and survive every situation. However, when we get trapped in the habit of being a certain way, when we allow this ego-self to remain attached to a known state of being, we restrict ourselves from expanding.

Unfortunately, it can be easy to remain identified with this conditioned character we allow and view ourselves to be. Remember, *you are not the character, you have a character*. If you want to move toward a new, more enjoyable way of living, you need to be willing to break free of this mental prison.

Think of it like this: Your authentic-self is the dreamer. Your ego-self is the person experiencing the dream. Never lose sight of who you truly are, even though you are living constantly through a character or identity. Strive to become more and more yourself, limitless and unbounded. Doing this will attract more and more of what you truly want.

To match the frequency of any new desired state, you need to be willing to let go of who you have been in order to shift into a truer version of yourself. Embodying your authentic-self is always a work in progress. The goal is never to achieve one masterful identity, but rather to be flexible at adjusting the identities you are embodying constantly (these are different for every area of your life), so you can become more and more of who you actually are.

Over time, we have each built up a collection of 'correct reactions' to events in our lives. Our emotional reactions determine the thoughts, perspectives, and beliefs we have about ourselves and our environment. We allow these reactions to define us—and as time passes, they become ever more entrenched in us, until we truly believe that they are who we are. We become comfortable with this definition of "self," even though it doesn't make us truly happy. At this point, you could say that our emotions have become our mind. The ego-self is in control.

Of course, as human beings, it's normal to have and experience the ego-self—possessing an ego-self is part of being human. However, a problem arises when we allow it to become the driving force of our existence. The ego-self's principal motivation is to keep us safe, so it's always on the lookout for things that might harm us … "Look out for this, watch out for that!" It's stuck back in cave-dweller self-protection mode, and its negative thoughts and emotions can start to define who we are—it is as if we walk through life wearing a mask that keeps us living in a "safe zone," rather than taking risks or making conscious choices about who we want to be. We must never forget that there is a truer, limitless, and authentic version of us behind the mask.

In a later chapter, we will learn to let go of our old habits, dis-identify with the ego-self, and embody an empowering version of ourselves. But for now, let's take a closer look at exactly what kind of thinking habits are causing our identification with the ego-self.

UNDERSTANDING YOUR ATTACHMENTS

Attachments are the ideas, concepts, and labels we cling to in order to defend the ego-self. It isn't necessary to detail the normal attachments people form, however, it is important to point out that not all attachments are obvious. Some attachments are limiting thoughts—and when you become attached to the contents of your mind, you are no longer free to think in any way that is different from the thoughts you've attached yourself to.

We form attachments—to both thoughts and things—to stay in control and to avoid suffering. It's a way of avoiding our fears, the process of change, and the unknown. The truth is, this is the exact behavior that causes resistance and stress in our lives.

Attachments, when they are challenged or lost, can cause immense suffering. We believe that without them, we lack something, and when we feel that way, we suffer. When we're grabbing on to these mental constructs with all our strength, how can we be open to receiving any new insight or inspiration to change our lives? To stay attached requires energy. Thus, when we are using our energy to cling to attachments, we are wasting energy that could have been used to build our dreams.

Therefore, it is important to inventory things you are attached to. Of course, each person is different. Below I provide a sample of standard, as well as less obvious attachments. This will give you a clue as to the types of attachments to look for in your own situation.

Standard Attachments:

- Possessions
- People and relationships
- Social status
- Financial status
- Ideology

Less Obvious Attachments:

- Emotional pattern attachments
- Habits of thinking
- Superiority complex (Narcissism)
- Inferiority complex (Victim mentality)
- Fear of change

The second list can be more difficult to deal with than the first, as these attachments tend to hide within the subconscious and sometimes even unconscious mind. When we develop emotional patterns and patterns of thought, we tend to identify with them because they are a normal part of our everyday experience. For example, if someone were to go through many negative events in a day, they might say that they had a 'bad day.' If this were to carry on for weeks and months on end, they could start to identify with the idea that they're 'unlucky.' Hence, they carry this general view of themselves every day, and as a result, they experience a lack of luck in their reality.

An example of a person being attached to emotional patterns might be someone who stays in an abusive relationship. Perhaps it is their attachment to the familiar, their fear of being alone, their fear of poverty, or their fear of being judged by others—there are many reasons a person stays in such a situation. One thing is certain though - it is fear that drives attachments. Being attached to something is usually grounded in our fear of an outcome we are trying to avoid. We fear experiencing lack.

The biggest problem with attachments—especially the less obvious ones—is that we can design a justification for each one. It's easy for the ego-self to control how you should think and feel if you're unable to separate yourself from its grasp. In a later chapter, we will address this issue further. For now, consider the attachments you have created for yourself. They're probably more numerous than you may have originally thought! A simple exercise to help you identify what attachments you have is included below.

Exercise: Attachment Discovery

Ask yourself the following questions regarding your attachments acknowledged in the previously provided lists:

- Would I be okay if I did not have this?
- Would I be okay with not achieving this goal the way I imagined it?
- Am I disturbed mentally or emotionally by the physical lack of this?

Ask yourself these questions, reflect on them… rewrite them to fit your specific experiences if you feel called to. When we shine a light on our attachments, we have already begun the process of detaching from them.

THE MEANING WE GIVE CIRCUMSTANCES

For the most part, it's not circumstances themselves that cause us to feel or think in a certain way. It's the meaning we attribute to circumstances that generates our state of being relative to them. When we do this, we cease to relate to the essence of an experience, instead, we relate to the label we give to it. In other words, we are not viewing circumstances as they really are, but as limited definitions based on conditioned assumptions. As we do this throughout our lives, we begin to create a world filled with definitions, without any deductive reasoning to support how each definition applies to any given circumstance.

Eventually, the illusory definitions you give to certain aspects of your life begin to support the others. As time goes on, you build a web of attachments, each strand linked to another, that justifies the meanings you have applied to them. For example, a situation where you are let go from work can make you feel unworthy of being in a loving relationship with someone. "Nobody wants to be with someone who is unemployed," the ego-self might say. While the reasoning behind this may sound logical, it is still an assumption. Being let go from work has nothing to do with your worthiness. Being unemployed has nothing to do with your connection with someone.

Now, this doesn't mean you should stop everything you're doing and assume things will magically work out. What *it* does mean is that you need to be aware of this web of attachments and disentangle from it. This way, you can avoid coming to conclusions unconsciously by using faulty reasoning. Think with more clarity. Assume less. Begin living more consciously. Focus on the parameters of each area of your life. Be less caught up in this energy-draining mess of attachments.

If we give meaning to a thing or situation, it becomes truth as far as we're concerned. As such, to us, the thoughts and emotions generated by that thing or circumstance are valid. Therefore, those things we view as positive will generate positive thoughts and emotions, and those we view as negative will have the opposite effect. But here's an interesting point: *Nothing has built-in meaning!* There are no universally designated labels that attribute specific meanings to people, places, items, or events. We create our own labels. This is why one person might find something tragic, while another person views the same situation as fortuitous. So, how do we deal with this? Check out the simple exercise below:

Exercise: The Lens of Positivity

When you experience any supposed negative circumstance in your life, see if you can look at it from a perspective that could generate a positive response from you. This will work more often when you turn it into a circumstance that is beneficial for you in some way. For example, let's say someone criticizes something you have created. Rather than reacting indignantly, imagine that the critique provides you with an opportunity to look at the situation differently. This new viewpoint may lead you to re-evaluate your original idea, which in turn may lead to a beneficial outcome for you. If not, at least you took the time to view your creation from a new perspective, giving yourself the opportunity to improve it if you could. Be open to exploring new perspectives.

When you practice this way of seeing things consistently, you will begin to switch your negative reactions to positive ones. This will serve to shift your vibrations toward a more harmonious frequency that eventually facilitates the manifestation process.

THE INFINITE VIEWS OF REALITY

Many eminent scientists have put forth the theory that we exist in a universal construct consisting of an infinite number of parallel realities—a multiverse. Without getting into the details of theoretical physics, let me explain. The predominant theory regarding our Universe is that it is ever expanding. Ironically, science is only now beginning to catch up on a description that has been known since ancient times. Both the ancient Greeks and early Buddhists had detailed explanations regarding this phenomenon—and modern science is just now beginning to prove the theory via mathematical means. In a nutshell, the theory states that there are innumerable different realities that exist parallel to one another. This number is increasing (in the direction of infinity) as the

Universe expands. But the most amazing part is that we are tied into these realities as opposed to being separate from them!

Our ability to perceive reality is more far reaching than most people can imagine. Why? Because we utilize our senses in ways that baffle those who live by standard biological precepts. Modern science is also just beginning to understand phenomena that lie beyond the five human senses—such things as so-called psychic abilities (ESP), near-death experiences (NDEs), and spiritually transformative experiences (STEs), etc. As such, we are constantly seeing reality as a 'flow' that moves throughout each moment in time. In essence, we are seeing a collection of frames that run one after another.

For example, imagine a deck of cards, with each card being almost the same as the ones on either side of it—there is only a tiny difference in each one. When you flip quickly through the cards, you get a 'moving' image created by a sequence of static frames. In this same manner, imagine that in our own everyday reality, we are viewing frames created within an infinite number of parallel realities, but each frame appears to be occurring in a single reality we call our life. But, in truth, our reality is an ever-flowing movement of perception—traveling through an expanding collection of frozen frames of separate realities.

This is extremely important to understand since knowledge of this fact can lead you to change your point of view (POV). You see, our perception of any reality is based on our ability to resonate with the vibrational frequency of that particular reality. This much science has already established. Once you change your POV, and emotionally resonate with it, you can change your frequency and access a completely different reality—and thereby experience a completely different outcome. Amazing! This shows us that while we may insist that the world (as we see it) is the only reality—it isn't.

When we have solidified this knowledge, we are one step closer to understanding just how practical it is to change our circumstances. We are moving toward what I refer to as the Three F's – Fulfillment, Flow, and Freedom.

"Reality is merely an illusion, albeit a very persistent one."
- Albert Einstein

HOW TO HANDLE MIXED EMOTIONS

I understand that a few readers may find the previous explanation difficult to grasp. Sometimes, it is hard to break down the concepts of quantum physics into easily understandable components. Don't worry. Occasionally, I'll offer up a few technical (or near-technical) explanations merely as reference points, to illustrate the logic behind what this book has to offer.

If something seems a bit vague, don't be concerned. Ultimately, this book is about practical ways to exercise control over your vibrational state. Controlling your vibration means mastering your thoughts and emotions so you can choose a path that leads to the best possible life for you. That said; let's look at how to handle the rollercoaster ride of our emotions.

When we were young, we were taught that life is filled with ups and downs; that we should savor the 'good stuff' and loath the 'bad stuff.' When we are delving into the magical possibilities of how the Laws of Manifestation can work for us in our lives, the ups and downs of life are going to present themselves to us in real time—and our job is to enjoy the ride—and make life's ups and downs work for us instead of against us.

> *"Life is like a roller coaster.*
> *You can either scream every time there is a bump*
> *or you can throw your hands up and enjoy the ride."*
> **- Unknown**

The term 'mixed emotions' refers to times we all experience when our emotions seem out of our control. In other words, they are emotions that have been conditioned to surface, uninvited, as a result of external circumstances.

Mixed emotions result from (once again) our beliefs, and from attaching our sense of worth, identity, or security to the people, places, and things we experience every day. Remember … there can be a major disconnect between theory and belief. We can spend a great deal of time learning about a new paradigm or description of reality; we can agree wholeheartedly with a premise that we read; and we might even try to convince others to subscribe to our new way of thinking. But that doesn't mean we can use our new knowledge to our own advantage readily.

To begin manifesting positive results consistently, you need to be aware of when you are acting from your conditioned beliefs and when you are acting from a conscious state. When you reflect on where you are coming from (what you are standing as), it will be obvious why your manifestation results tend to look like a rollercoaster ride. You can be standing as either your body, mind, or awareness. Refer to the following diagram for clarity:

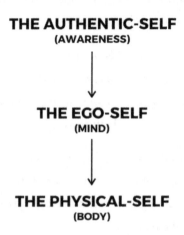

THE AUTHENTIC-SELF
(AWARENESS)

↓

THE EGO-SELF
(MIND)

↓

THE PHYSICAL-SELF
(BODY)

When we manifest success unconsciously, we are doomed to lose it. This is why one's life can exhibit misery, success … misery, success, etc. Instead of making a breakthrough, you are merely paying the endless fare on your own personal rollercoaster! There's a name for this frequency. It's called 'feeling stuck.' This happens when you choose to allow your conditioned ego-self to tell you how to think, feel, and act in relation to a given set of circumstances based on the attachments it has. Your thoughts, feelings, and actions need to be conscious choices. When we make conscious choices, we practice the art of conscious living: A state in which we get to choose the reality we want to live from—the desired future. Fortunately, as you shall see soon, this is not as difficult as it sounds.

Exercise: Redefining Your Beliefs

Here is a simple exercise I like to call 'The Why?' exercise. It's designed to point out the reasons behind the emotions you feel. Too often, we allow our actions to be driven by subconscious emotional responses without considering the underlying cause of the emotion in the first place. Once the curtain has been drawn back to reveal the actual cause of an emotion, it becomes a relatively simple matter to change it. After all, as noted earlier, none of us like being held prisoner in a jail with imaginary bars—right? No one wants to be ordered around by a jailor they cannot even see.

When you come face-to-face with your beliefs, perspectives, and emotions, you will have the opportunity to question their validity. In other words, ask yourself, "Do they deserve the energy I'm allowing them to have?" You'll notice that there is an underlying theme in this exercise. Since the Universe contains everything (except lack), if an emotion is based on a reason involving lack—then the emotion must be coming from conditioned assumptions of reality.

In order to complete this exercise, take a few minutes and write down the emotions that revolve around things that are troubling you. Then, under each emotion, write what you feel is the reason for that emotion. (Be sure to answer each question emotionally, not rationally. Do not *think* it through, *feel* it.) Then continue breaking down the reasons until you find the underlying cause of that emotion. If you like, get someone you trust to partner with you. It can help to have someone else ask the questions so you can focus on the answers. Here is an example:

Emotion: I'm feeling depressed.

> Q: Why?
> A: Because I hate my job.
>
> Q: Why don't you leave the job?
> A: Because then I would have no money.

Then continue with the line of questioning.

> Q: Why would you have no money?
> A: Because I would not have a job.
>
> Q: Why couldn't you get another job?
> A: Because I don't believe I can get another job.
>
> Q: Why do you believe you can't get another job?
> A: Because nobody would want to hire me.
>
> Q: Why would nobody hire you?
> A: Because I don't feel worthy enough.
>
> Q: Why do you not feel worthy?
> A: Because my father used to tell me I'm not worthy.

There—that's your key point. The last answer in this example shows that an external perspective is affecting your internal perspective. So, focus on this point—see it for what it is. In order to reshape the reality of being stuck in a job that does not fulfill you, you need to begin shifting away from this hidden belief. Now, pair up the original emotion (depression) with that last statement and you'd have:

I am depressed because my father used to tell me I'm not worthy.

You see, when you are in alignment, you exude abundance and live through your desires. You no longer chase your desires or limit yourself to what you want. Instead, you become attractive to the thing you want, and what you want actually begins to chase you. When you shine a light on a limiting belief, it loses its power—and it becomes clear exactly which perspective you need to work on. Not yet convinced? There is one more thing you can do. Ask yourself a final question:

Q: How does this belief serve to satisfy my ego-self?

When we choose to hold on to a certain belief, it's because there is something about that belief that makes us feel secure. This is true even in cases in which we are punishing ourselves with that belief. In this case, some reasons for clinging on to a belief might be:

- I don't want others to see me fail.
- I don't want to lose the approval of my parents and loved ones.
- I don't want my significant other to suffer from my losses.

The problem here is that you will continue manifesting and attracting the exact circumstances that match the reasonings of the ego-self, even though the reality you are experiencing isn't what you want at all.

The belief system we have each created/subscribed to, defines who we are, provides what we need for protection, and makes us feel safe and comfortable—we feel good. Even unfounded and negative beliefs hold the potential of false security. In this case, false security comes in the form of:

- being in control
- having money
- being loved and respected by others.

When you look at things from this perspective, it is easy to see why some people stay in abusive relationships or get stuck in well-paying jobs that do not fulfill them. We manifest circumstances not because we want them, but because we were told that is what we deserve or should have in order to be 'successful.' It's like placing a bandage on a wound that really needs stitches. On the surface, everything may look fine. But underneath, nothing will ever heal properly. Consider the surface of the bandage to be what you're showing to the world and what's underneath it to be what you really feel.

Once you discover the underlying beliefs that stand in the way of you being able to manifest with alignment, then you can allow yourself to let it go. This will come from a different perspective that reflects who you really are and where you should ultimately be focused. (More on this in Chapter Four).

The ego-self will always want to take charge, place arbitrary meaning onto your reality, and define it as quickly as possible so that there is reference. Once there is a reference, there is a way to manipulate and control this aspect of reality. Without this control, the ego-self suffers. The identity dwindles and it begins to lose more of itself. When we dis-identify with the mind and physical reality, we enter the state of 'No Mind' (*Mushin*), and we begin to witness reality for what it really is: an illusion.

"If you use your mind to study reality, you won't understand either your mind or reality. If you study reality without your mind, you'll understand both."

- **Bodhidharma**

The more conscious we become of the ego-self and its underhanded tactics, the more consciously we can create the reality we actually want. Before making decisions or coming to conclusions about your life, you always want to ask yourself the question: "*Who am I standing as?*" Are you standing as the human body, the ego-self, or your soul? Recognize and notice the differences between each. Once you do, you can become more efficient in your journey to creating a life that deeply fulfills you.

CHAPTER THREE

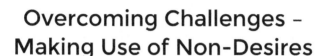

Overcoming Challenges – Making Use of Non-Desires

Every single day of our lives, we are met with some sort of challenge. The challenges we experience fall within a wide range of complexity. Some are small and easy to deal with; others are big and require more thought. A person can have the challenge of figuring out what to eat for lunch and within the same day, have the challenge of breaking up with their partner. Regardless of the challenges we face, what determines the outcomes is how we respond to them. In this chapter, we're going to cover how to overcome challenges effectively in order to get the most out of them. We will discover why people tend to hold on to the negative, even when it's abundantly clear that it's a mistake to do so. I'm going to show you the reasons it can be easy to make the same life mistakes over and over, and thus continue manifesting unnecessary challenges.

When you see the less-than-ideal events in your life for what they truly are—stepping stones to living the life you desire—you'll be ready to use them to your advantage, rather than as a reason to feel sorry for yourself or your situation. This chapter probably contains the single-most important message for you in this book: When you understand how the reality of challenges works, in an amazingly short period, you will find yourself witnessing a complete change in your life. Instead of stumbling back and forth on a road filled with the same pitfalls and roadblocks, you will see a new, clear path that leads toward the effortless manifestation of your desires. It all starts when we understand, accept, and live by Principle #3.

PRINCIPLE #3:
Contrast and Challenges
Are Always Beneficial.

NO EXPERIENCE IS EVER LIMITING

Throughout my life, I've come to understand that there is no such thing as a life-limiting experience. In truth, any challenge we face (which at first may seem like a life-limiting experience) leads us to a brand-new chapter in our lives. By perceiving experiences as negative, we buy into an illusion—and unfortunately, people do this every day.

Once illusions have been set aside, we see behind the veil of so-called 'negative' experiences. When we encounter something we perceive as negative (or positive), there is always something more to learn. This shows us that experiences are designed for us to learn from—not to dwell on mentally or emotionally. We are meant to gain the knowledge we need and leave the rest behind. Once we understand this, we can become aware of the underlying causes of, and the effects of, each of our experiences.

Fear of experiencing a potentially negative outcome often arises in our lives, so we avoid stepping into a new reality and facing new challenges. Overcoming this initial fear of challenges is an essential first step. Once we get over this hurdle, growth becomes inevitable. Often, external discomfort is necessary so we can break free of the jail of unconscious internal dissatisfaction. As mentioned previously, since we are manifesting constantly, we are manifesting both benefits and detriments. There could be times in which we manifest challenges consciously because they are the best next experience we need to have (or to overcome) so that we can evolve. For example, if your desire is to be a more skillful artist, your best next experience would be to learn and master new artistic skills.

However, a lot of the time, such challenges (or obstacles) are manifested unconsciously, because we are still clinging to deeply rooted beliefs and attachments. These sorts of challenges often serve as a redirection tool to steer you back onto the path that is most fulfilling to you. When we accept challenges for what they truly are (a catalyst for growth), we're more open to self-reflection, and thus, more effective optimal learning. Our best teacher is our own personal experience.

Taking responsibility for and accepting our personal manifestations (no matter how they come) gives us power. It allows us to embody the truth that ultimately, we create our own reality. We do not control reality per se, but because we can change how we respond to the reality we are experiencing, we can redirect our life in the general direction we want to go, and as a result, change our reality. Practicing this gives us significantly more response-ability. So, we can ask ourselves, "How can I respond positively to this supposed negative experience?" In other words, "How can I benefit from this experience?" When we ask these questions, we improve our relationship with ourselves and with our surroundings, thus falling back into (and finding) alignment.

Exercise: Developing Greater Responsibility

In this exercise, we will be uncovering the parts of your life you could be avoiding, pushing aside, or neglecting, simply because of your fear of facing them. This can express itself in the form of blaming others, playing the victim, or even ignoring parts completely because of how much emotional turmoil is involved. To discover areas in your life in which you can take on more responsibility, ask yourself these questions:

- Am I rejecting this moment in order to experience the next?
- Am I avoiding something in my life? What am I avoiding?
- Do I blame others for where I am? Whom do I blame?
- Do I place responsibility on others for any area of my life? On whom do I place it? And in which area?
- Do I feel like I am not in control of an area of my life? Which area?

Taking back responsibility is not meant to overwhelm you. It is a form of taking back your power and energy and not allowing situations to take it from you. Remember, we are not trying to put more on our plate; instead, we are trying to improve our ability to respond to situations when they arise from a mindful and conscious state. This way, we can protect the state of being we want to be living through.

If you are feeling limited in some way right now, there is usually a belief around a perceived limitation. I say "perceived limitation" because each experience in our lives gives us an opportunity to view it in a limitless way. The key is to take a perceived obstacle and look at it with an unlimited mind. This means you can choose to view yourself as a source of abundance rather than a source of limitation. When we feel 'stuck' in undesirable life circumstances, for example, it can mean one of two things: Either we are unaware of the many opportunities around us or we are afraid of seizing these opportunities because they represent the unknown (and the unknown is the enemy of the ego).

NAVIGATING THE UNKNOWN AND NON-DESIRES

"We do not fear the unknown.
We fear what we think we know about the unknown."
- Teal Swan

The greatest reason people fear the unknown is that the unknown is where we begin making our own choices. Venturing into the unknown requires that you take responsibility for how you navigate your life—and taking responsibility is difficult for some (if not most) people. Throughout our lives, we have allowed others to make our choices for us, either consciously or unconsciously. We are told to follow a path that may be 'good' for us from the perspective of others, but most of the time, that is not true for us—nor is it what we truly want. These choices are conditioned into us—and eventually, they affect our subconscious mind, tricking us into believing someone else's version of what is right and what is wrong.

Understanding this alone should be enough to inspire in you a sense of awe and anticipation of the new life that stretches before you. However, the other side of the coin is that now you have a choice ... you can start taking full responsibility for your life, or you can choose to allow the decision-making process to make you fearful (and potentially, paralyzingly nervous).

Most people approach manifestation like a nervous swimmer who wants to jump into the pool, but avoids the diving board—they dip their toes in first, then their ankles, etc. Once they're immersed in the water, however, they enjoy the weightless effort of swimming toward their goals.

But here's a critical point: You can't compensate for a lack of vibrational resonance simply with physical action. You may make all the right moves, but the end result will not be what you're looking for if you are not a vibrational match with the end result you want. This is what you see with so many people who are desperately following the steps attributed to the Laws of Manifestation. This is also why two people can take the exact same actions and get completely different results. The key here is to move forward towards your dreams with not just your actions, but also with clarity on where you are *going* and who you are *being*. When you apply these two first, the *doing* will come naturally.

Someone can make sure that all their 'tools' (journals, vision boards, etc.) are in place. They can place pictures of their desires all around them. They can read all the appropriate books on the subject of manifestation. At the end of it all, however, they end up disappointed that the Laws of Manifestation supposedly just do not work for them. When we desperately need, chase, or place excess importance on our goals, or make excessive efforts to achieve them, we are actually building resistance against them. Someone who is whole, fulfilled, eager, excited, and in alignment isn't looking for results. The results are in their everyday experience of becoming and manifesting. The manifestation is the natural result of them being *process oriented*.

It's important to remember that the Universe has no limitations. Therefore, what we deem to be the 'unknown' also has no limitations. It contains all of our desires—even desires that we are not yet aware of. But the unknown also contains something else: what can be called our non-desires. When we are focusing on what we *don't* want, or seeking to avoid manifesting our non-desires, the Universe perceives that as a valid option for creation. The Universe does not care about the *meaning* you give your thoughts, but the *content* of them. In other words, saying "I want this car" or "I don't want this car," sends the same signal. Putting your focus on avoiding an experience will only lead to more of it. If you give energy to *lack*, or you focus on all the reasons why abundance *isn't* showing itself in physical form, the Universe will be more than pleased to hand more of that to you.

But there is a way to avoid this pitfall. Some call it "unbending intent." It boils down to committing to entering the unknown with no doubts and an unshakable confidence. Your conviction must be unwavering when it comes to changing your reality for the better. One way to assist with this is to ask yourself this question daily: "Am I devoted to spending the rest of my life in a limited fashion—or am I committed to changing my reality for the better by making my inner reality reflect where I want to be, no matter what?"

If your answer is "Yes, I'm committed to changing my reality," this new viewpoint brushes aside doubts you may have been holding on to when facing the unknown. Now, you have accepted what may lie beyond your comfort zone. You have committed to thinking outside the box. It is no longer a question of whether you're going swimming in that pool. It's a question of what you'll be doing when you're in it. Challenges and obstacles will arise, but this is only because you are being tested. Use this experience to your benefit and grow with it. Doubts are now just a waste of time.

PHYSICAL REALITY DELAY

We are living in a world that can work actively against conscious manifestation. As our technology advances, we come to expect that things—from communication to entertainment—will come to us with increased speed. This expectation comes at a cost:

limited attention spans, impatience, and frustration. Often, people give up on their dreams prematurely, believing that "If it hasn't come yet, it never will." But these people are overlooking a critical factor: they misunderstand how manifestation works.

Our greatest manifestation obstacle can be overcome by a simple change in perspective. You see, at any given moment, we can only perceive a single reality—this solid physical world. Of course, we know that underneath our perception of this 'solid' reality, lies an invisible field of vibration and energy that is always in flux. Thus, in order to move from one reality to another requires a vibrational adjustment. If this were not the case, our world would be filled with sorcerers who could make things appear out of thin air. While there are accounts of advanced yogi masters who can do this on a limited basis, we don't generally run into them in our day-to-day lives. (It's lucky we don't live in a fantasy movie—imagine the chaos!)

Since most of us are not able to make things appear out of the blue, it's important to realize that we need to move through other parallel realities to reach the one we desire—and as we do this, there is an inevitable time delay. If we wish to continue on the path toward our ultimate, desired reality, we must maintain our composure by doing this one simple thing: We must assign less importance to the physical world.

As each circumstance in our lives reveals itself, it is vital that we move in harmony with what we want to be experiencing on a moment-to-moment basis, regardless of what appears in front of us—and regardless of what has happened in a similar situation in the past. We need to deal with every challenge we face in our lives consciously in the here and now, being mindful and aware, without referring to past experiences or societal assumptions for guidance or direction. Embody the future you want to experience.

We must also be mindful of keeping our emotions under control. Why? Because it is easy to let our emotional reactions to any current situation be based on experience. If we let our primitive five senses (seeing, hearing, feeling, smelling, and touching) control us, instead of controlling them, we may find ourselves making the same decisions and attracting the same things over and over again. Giving an excess of meaning to a single snapshot from your emotional past creates internal resistance to what is right now. This is one of the main reasons people give up on the manifestation process—because they *think* they are stuck.

DREAM, CHALLENGE, MANIFEST

When all is said and done, manifestation can be broken down into a three-step process. When you understand its foundation, you will have a broader perspective of how it all works—and a deeper understanding of why your former concept of physical-world reality is no longer relevant. The three steps are:

- **Dream –**

  You make a decision to create something and to live in a different reality than the one you are currently living in. This leads to new insights, opportunities, or experiences that you never considered or expected. Because of this, you see that your imagination deserves your full attention and unwavering intent. The results of this focus on your imagination will justify the energy you have placed on it.

- ## Challenge –

    Imagine the Universe asking you, "Do you really want it?" It's a question you need to ask yourself too. Considering this question might seem like a roadblock to getting what you want, but it isn't—instead, it is a stepping stone. If this self-questioning step didn't exist, we would be overwhelmed with the good and bad things we manifest. So, filter your wants and desires by asking yourself, "Do I really want it?" If you really desire something, answering this question with an enthusiastic "Yes!" will create the initial momentum needed to overcome and learn from every challenge ahead of you.

- ## Manifest –

    This is when you've reached your desired "goal." You've held a frequency consistently through a multitude of parallel realities, and you've reached the one that you desired to resonate with vibrationally. This is when your imagination is reflected in physical form.

Throughout this process, you have known that the time frame required to reach your goal is related directly to the amount of energy and commitment you have applied to achieving that goal. Generally, the energy output boils down to the amount of energy needed to shift from one parallel reality to another. Put simply, moving into a reality in which someone remembers to get you a cake for your birthday is a far cry from a reality in which you're chosen to be the CEO of a major corporation. But never become discouraged. BOTH realities exist in the Universe!

TURN CHALLENGES INTO ADVANTAGES

There is a simple yet powerful way to shift your mindset in relation to your everyday experiences. But it takes a bit more than just paying lip service to a given concept. For example, any life coach will tell you that "You don't have problems, you have challenges." However, taking the leap from perceiving a challenge as a seemingly unsolvable problem to perceiving it as a learning opportunity takes a paradigm shift. There is a huge difference between knowing something in theory and internalizing it into a belief or way of living. Here is an exercise to help you do just that.

Exercise: Challenge Reflection

The way to make this shift is to remember that the mind and body cannot distinguish the difference between imagination and actual physical experience. It can help to reflect on how you handled past situations. Let's begin by doing the following three practices.

1. Write down a time in your life when you were rewarded for overcoming a challenge in a seemingly negative situation successfully.
2. Write down a few examples of important lessons you learned (or should have learned) from experiencing a seemingly negative situation.
3. Write down a time in your life when something bad that happened was a result of your reactive and low vibrational state. How would things have gone differently if you had responded consciously?

You can gain a lot of clarity, insight, and experience from reflecting on experiences and looking at life objectively. Asking yourself such questions works on two levels. You'll practice seeing aspects of your life without making assumptions or having conditioned reactions. When you reach a stage in which you can understand and anticipate the results of your vibrational state, the manifestation process will become clear. You'll begin to see cause-and-effect relationships and you'll begin to anticipate how your actions, feelings, and deeds produce certain outcomes. You'll see how any given 'negative' situation didn't just 'happen' to you. You'll realize what it is you've really been asking for, by way of your subconscious mind. Your foresight will be 20-20, not just your hindsight. Eventually, you'll need to counteract some of these 'requests' that have plagued you throughout your life.

LEARNING FROM YOUR CHALLENGES

One of the simplest, most effective ways to learn from experience is through this equation: *Repetition + Intensity*. Repetition is how we gain reference experience, while intensity is how we remember this reference experience. It's the same in sports: Repetition builds the muscle memory needed to excel in physical activities. Similarly, in martial arts, the repetition of one single skill is what separates an expert from a novice.

"I fear not the man who has practiced 10,000 kicks once,
but I fear the man who has practiced one kick 10,000 times."
- Bruce Lee

When working in any particular career field, the "repetition + intensity" formula allows us to move past the basics so that we can hone the finer skills of our profession. We can also use this formula to shift away from an older way of thinking and make room for a newer way that will serve us better.

Here is where we encounter another obstacle that many people struggle with. Different people have different concepts of what it means to employ repetition. For those who are well-disciplined, being able to dedicate themselves to consistently repeating an action is simply a part of who they are. However, for others, there is an obvious struggle to continue breaking free from the old paradigm. This is where intensity plays a massive role.

Intensity is not based on the amount of effort you made, struggle you endured, or action you took. It is based on how much you were able to learn in order to embody the new you. The more you taste the feeling of freedom, confidence, and joy, the easier it will be to replicate it. Now this can only be done by pushing past your comfort zone. You never want to put yourself in a dangerous situation, however. You want to put yourself in a situation that is just uncomfortable enough to challenge the old you.

"Own your fear, and lean just beyond it, in every aspect of your life."
- David Deira

Case in point: An untold number of people have attempted to play a musical instrument in their lives, but have never succeeded. Why? Because for one reason or another, they didn't practice enough—or in the right way. After all, practice does not make perfect—practice makes permanent. Of course, this is simply an analogy—we're not really talking about taking piano or tuba lessons here. We're talking about playing consciously with our thoughts and emotions so we can manifest better circumstances in our lives. Not a second goes by when you are not thinking or feeling—even when you are asleep or unconscious. When you are living unconsciously, you are unknowingly building up a reservoir of conditioned thoughts and feelings. In fact, this way of living has become a habit for most people. As a result, living consciously often feels like effort. It took many years to fill your cup, so it does not make sense to expect yourself to empty it in a few days. That said, emptying your cup can be a much faster process—especially if you are committed to doing the internal work the right way and consistently.

Most of us have big dreams. With our big dreams come big challenges—and big changes. When we make consistent attempts to change our lives, the old energy (usually in the form of beliefs, emotions, and relationships) will hinder your attempt to change. Both internal and external forces will try to prevent you from changing. Not only are you stepping into the unknown, but others in your life are also stepping into it with you. Throughout your life, you've established a notion of who you are in relation to the energy within and around you. When you attempt to stop the cycle, rewrite the pattern, or modify the programming, there is always a little pull back, because you are changing a habit … and often, habits cannot be changed easily.

Many people you know will not understand these concepts (as simple as they are), and will have nothing to say that resonates with where you want to go. They might say, "It sounds crazy." Maybe they will even warn you not to get involved with "woo woo" or "sorcery." As we'll talk about in a later chapter, that's okay. There's no need to impose your newfound beliefs on others, or to get defensive—simply accept that other people have different journeys, and continue to develop yours.

Your goal is not to convince the world of your truth. Your goal is firstly to become aware of your own conditioned misconceptions, secondly, to use repetition + intensity to un-memorize them, and finally, to replace them with the truth: *your truth*.

CRYSTALLIZING A NEW PERSPECTIVE

When it comes to transforming their lives, many people intellectualize a new idea but neglect to incorporate those ideas into their belief systems. In my life, for example, I have met countless people who can restate the metaphysical and manifestation philosophies they have learned from attending countless seminars and reading numerous books—but their knowledge remains superficial; they never really absorb it into their awareness as wisdom.

Learning new perspectives that resonate with us will always give us that initial jolt of excitement. It's as if we have found the missing piece of a puzzle. "Now that I know this concept, everything will change." At least, that's how most people think. But the truth is, after something is learned, if it is not applied consistently, it is mere knowledge and fails to transform into wisdom. This leads us naturally to always looking for the next 'new teaching.' If we truly want to become a master of the concepts we learn, we need to apply these concepts and learn from what we have applied. Asking yourself the following questions can help:

- How and where can I apply these teachings in my life?
- What mistakes did I make when applying these teachings?
- What lessons can I learn from my mistakes?
- How can I refine and improve upon my application of these teachings?

Apply a teaching, in the right way, until it becomes a part of who you are; a part of your belief system. Now … what exactly is a belief system?

Belief systems are a collection of crystallized perspectives. In other words, a belief system is composed of multiple views of manifold aspects of life that are repeated, solidified, and fortified with emotional involvement. What does this mean? It goes like this. The more you adhere stubbornly to doing something necessary to create the reality you want to experience, the more results you will see. When you 'toss away' any need for it to happen or you place excess importance upon a certain outcome or pathway, the evidence begins to accumulate even faster. Keep your emotional responses steady—positive but unattached to outcomes. Base your knowledge on the evidence you've now seen, and your knowledge becomes an ingrained belief. Lather, rinse, repeat.

Ironically, those who tend to keep things simple are the ones who tend to have the least difficulty when it comes to altering their reality. This is expressed through the principle of parsimony (Occam's Razor). This principle says that "entities should not be multiplied without necessity." In other words, the best next step, most of the time, is the simplest one.

When you begin to live through your new perspective, and the more you talk to people, take actions, and make decisions based on that new perspective, the more you'll ingrain new patterns into your subconscious. If you want to experience a new life, your new perspective needs to become your new way of living. Once you begin living for the future and you are no longer living from your past or current reality, changes will start manifesting. There is no magical formula involved. Manifestation is easy once you adopt a new perspective—and then let go and allow it to come to fruition naturally.

DEALING WITH PEOPLE WHO PRESENT CHALLENGES

When I wrote the subtitle above, I smiled. If one were to believe all the things written on this topic over the years, this section could span an entire library! Dealing with difficult people is simple, but not always easy. Conditioned thoughts and emotions arise more frequently and with more intensity when we find ourselves engaging with another person or within a group of people. If we allow ourselves to fall victim to patterns that drain our energy (conflict, anger, jealousy, etc.), we'll waste it, and as a result, we'll have less energy to apply to our new intentions for a new reality. So, to conserve your energy for this task, you'll need to simplify your interactions with others. Here are five points to improve your interactions with others:

- When you encounter difficult people, react positively. It is being defensive that makes such people 'difficult' in the first place. Reacting negatively to difficult people is your choice, not theirs. Flip the script of your usual reaction. If you would normally react with anger, turn it into humor.

- Accept and respect another person's right to have free will—even if you disagree.

- Your communication with others should remain clear and honest—and above all, what you say should mirror your true intentions.

- Trying to control others is a waste of time. Controlling yourself is the only thing worth your time.

- There is no need for drama. In fact, when we apply the principle of parsimony, this is exactly what we get—an effective, simple solution to managing our state of being relative to those around us.

When you show up consciously in your interactions, people will sense security and confidence within you. The most influential and charismatic leaders of our time are always present when they engage with others. When you give another person your presence, often, this is enough to get them to stop wanting to clash with you.

YOU'RE NOT DOING THINGS 'WRONG'

We live in a society that applies the concepts of 'winning' and 'losing' to everything. Just consider the age-old saying about the acquisition of material goods: "He who dies with the most toys wins." While the saying is meant to be ironic and comedic, there is a great amount of belief that backs it up.

From the time we were in grade school, we were given tests on which we were graded somewhere between "excellent" and "failed." The classes we attended demanded that we focus on passing these tests according to arbitrary parameters. These ideas of what denotes success and failure are diamond-etched into our subconscious minds. While these tests may have served to motivate us to study hard and work toward certain achievements, they also might have created a devastating obstacle that led us to believe that we were not where we should have been. The fact is: We are always exactly where we need to be.

When we define where we are as somewhere we shouldn't be, we drop back down into the frequency of what is. In other words, we attach ourselves vibrationally to our current physical reality— we emanate a frequency of doubt and worry. When there is doubt in our creation process, we become less likely to take action or think thoughts and feel feelings that match with our desired reality. Similarly, when we notice that things aren't manifesting in the way we wish they would, we get into a cycle of looking for what's wrong so we can stop doing it—and again, we start to resonate with *what is-ness*. In other words, we attach ourselves vibrationally to what we don't want … and emanate a frequency of uncertainty and fear. The temptation to look for what is wrong (instead of what is right) is a direct reflection of the "fear of failure" rooted in past conditioning.

It should be clear by now that expecting instant gratification for your intentions is a rookie mistake. Do not doubt the effectiveness of what you're doing, especially if you are feeling more empowered in relation to how you respond to life. Remain unattached to circumstances and outcomes, while at the same time placing your focus on moving toward your excitement and what you want. Remember, you get confirmation that you're on the right track when you get a positive answer to the question: *Who am I becoming?*

CHAPTER FOUR

The Roadmap to Happiness – Following Your Most Fulfilling Path

What does it take to be truly happy? How do we find satisfaction and joy in everyday circumstances? Where do we go to find happiness, satisfaction, and joy?

Since the beginning of this book, I've been hinting at the idea of manifesting with authenticity. In other words, choosing a path that is true to you; not choosing a path other people say you should take or that others have found success on. Finding your own path is about tapping into your inner truth—for when we look at the bigger context, it's the only one that really exists.

If you were to follow the path of someone else's truth, you'd never really tap into your authentic potential for living a life of purpose and fulfillment. A life well lived is one that, deep down, you truly enjoyed living—not the one with the most money, relationships, or status. That's where this next principle comes in.

PRINCIPLE #4:
Follow Your Truth. It's the Only One.

This principle deals with defining your personal roadmap to happiness. Unfortunately, many of us are expected to adhere to a pathway to happiness that someone else has defined for us. We are bombarded constantly with images that speak of certain accepted expectations and the results they lead to. For example, we're told that going to school to become a doctor and ending up with a high-paying career, huge home, etc. is the yardstick by which we should measure our happiness and success. If that particular path doesn't appeal to you, however, there are many more just like it—they just have different names and labels. From the time we're very young, we're trained to believe that our path to happiness is the one that satisfies everyone else's expectations: "I want to be an engineer," "I want to be a lawyer," etc. Most of the time, these pathways are based on earning income that will lead to financial security and a certain status within society.

Our loved ones almost never ask us: "What would you like to do that would make you happy?" A lot of the time, we do not even consider doing what makes us truly happy—in fact, we are accustomed to finding personal happiness through satisfying other's expectations and standards. Although in the short term we may reap some positive benefit from doing this, over the longer term, doing what someone else wants us to do only makes our authenticity and our inner desires want to burst out of us.

In this chapter, we'll take a look at how to generate positive emotions that resonate with your inner desires. When you are on the path to what you are truly meant to be or do, abundance becomes a given. You see, abundance isn't defined solely by following a certain path or achieving a certain level of material wealth. It is also defined by the positive emotions generated when we embrace and connect with our authentic-self. In other words, abundance isn't a reward for following a pre-approved path—it is the natural result of resonating with what makes us truly happy! Therefore, happiness is not a reward; it's a natural product of our authentic vibrational frequency. It's with this frequency that you become attractive to that which you want to attract. Let's take a closer look at this.

> *"Happiness is when what you think, what you say,*
> *and what you do are in harmony."*
> **- Mahatma Gandhi**

LIGHTING THE FIRE WITHIN

Most of us have heard expressions such as, "Follow your joy" or "Follow your dreams." However, it may be difficult to imagine doing this, since we're taught that there is a narrow path to achieving even the basics in life, such as being self-sufficient and paying our bills. You will always be presented with a challenge, regardless of whether you are in perfect alignment. However, some challenges are worth more than others. Often, we limit ourselves to the basics, and this is okay in the short term, especially if you are in a life-or-death situation. Survival comes first. But when you are blessed enough to have the chance to think about the next stage of your life, you should take it.

Always have in store a grander vision for how you want to live over the long term. This is what will get you jumping out of bed excited, inspired, and eager to create and live a magical life. If we stay too focused on the basics, this is where our energy goes, and as a result, we will keep on creating this constant need and struggle for it. *To dream small and dream big take the same amount of energy.* Give yourself permission to think bigger and more ambitious thoughts. This grander vision should never be just a wish, but something you consistently intend to live for and through.

The perspectives I'm going to be talking about here hold true whether you're a physician or you work in a grocery store, and whether you have been married for thirty years or have been dating someone for two months. Any career or lifestyle choice a person makes can misalign them with their truth. Remember, the abundance we want to manifest comes from tapping into the thoughts and emotions that put us into alignment.

How often have we seen examples of people who started off with virtually nothing and suddenly become prominent in society? I guarantee you; they did not accomplish this by insisting on sacrificing their alignment so they could pay the bills. In other words, they did not define their experience based on limited goals and false desires. The manifestations of those things were a side effect of them following their truth. They aimed for the moon and landed among the stars. Throughout their journey, rather than resonating with their external experience, they were prioritizing

MANIFESTING WITH ALIGNMENT

alignment, being who they wanted to be, and tuning into the frequency of what they truly desired. Often, we find ourselves stuck because our decisions, or lack of decisions, are based on assumptions or faulty reasoning. The worst decision you can make when it comes to following your dreams is to not make a decision at all. Let's break down this idea even more.

There are three manifestor archetypes: unconscious manifestors, conscious manifestors, and authentic manifestors. Here is a brief explanation of each:

1. The unconscious manifestor: This person moves with the flow of their conditions. In other words, they are a product of their environment. They fail to create their own reality and allow other people and circumstances to do it for them.

2. The egoic manifestor: This person moves with the flow of their ego-self. They learn manifestation in an attempt to simply and only *get* and *take*. The end goal is to impress others, increase their sense of self-worth, and climb the hierarchy of society. They are never satisfied and only think about having more, especially when the identity of the ego-self is challenged.

3. The conscious manifestor: This person moves with the flow of their soul. They are clear about who they are and what they want. Their driving force comes from within and has nothing to do with external rules. Their goal is to find satisfaction in the process of becoming a truer version of themselves. The character they play is flexible and limitless. They are not bounded by definitions, assumptions, or expectations placed on them from the outside world.

All human beings are a mixture of all three archetypes because of the complexity and variation of the circumstances within our lives. However, if we truly want to live the life of our dreams, we need to let go of what we think this looks like based on external ideas and concepts. We need to look within. Only then can we find the answers we are looking for.

Here is the key point. The process I'm outlining for you here is an emotional process—not a rational one. It involves learning to recognize impulses and following them, thus embodying more of your authentic-self. Moving in this direction actually involves less resistance than you might imagine. In fact, internally, when you are following what your soul craves, there is no resistance. That's because when you move forward on this path, the Universe steps in immediately to give you a hand. When you're following the path that leads to more of your authentic expression, challenges turn into stepping stones.

The only resistance you may allow yourself to experience is that of the external world projecting its judgment and opinions onto who you are being and your external circumstances. As you follow your soul's path, you may feel a little bit of resistance at first. It feels uncomfortable because it is a process of disrupting disharmony. Remember, doing what others want you to do may lead to external satisfaction (e.g., having a great income or status), but it will never satisfy the internal longing of the soul. This is not to say that when you follow your soul, you will not have the great income or status. In fact, the more authentic you are, the more these things come to you with ease. The Universe will support those who support their authentic-self and that of others. In the next subchapter, we'll touch on how to tune into this path.

Before we do, heed this warning: Following what brings you happiness and joy is not the same as following what you find easy or familiar. As you may recall, the ego-self loves to stick to what it finds familiar. This is why it's important to let go of old, reactive behaviors and desires. I'll show you how to do this by *reframing* your desires and wants. Once you put these old impulses aside and replace them with a desire to move toward that which fulfills and benefits you the most, magic will begin to happen.

ALIGNING WITH YOUR AUTHENTIC-SELF

At this point, you may be wondering, "But where can I find my *truest* desires?" This is understandable, since nearly all of us are handed a limited list of choices when we are young. For example, we can imagine a small boy who is asked if he wants to be a doctor, an engineer, or a police officer. Or, a little girl who is given a list of choices that contains nurse, secretary, or school teacher. Don't get me wrong. All these are valid—but only to those people that truly and deeply resonate with them.

For those who may ask where they can find their 'truest desires,' the answer, fortunately, is simple. You don't have to try out everything under the sun until you stumble upon the one that's right for you. Follow what excites you the most *now* and correct course when a new, more exciting path appears. This does not mean getting distracted or unfocused with everything around you, but rather, using up all the excitement you have for one path, and when this withers, making the intention of being open to taking a new opportunity and moving in a new direction. Never sacrifice your dreams—aim to create a life that satisfies what your soul craves.

Each one of us has an authentic-self that wants to express itself in a unique way. These unique soul cravings will come in a variety of shapes, colors, and forms, so do not become rigid or attached to one path. Be open to changing direction if that is what your excitement is telling you.

No matter what path you choose, and no matter what level of material rewards you acquire, if you disregard the intentions of your authentic-self, you will always have a sense that something is missing. All too often, people become 'successful' professionals, but are plagued constantly by emotional and relationship troubles. On the surface, these people look as though they have 'everything in the world,' but underneath, they are suffering. Often, the goals we commit to in order to meet the expectations of others and 'fill our role' in society can be called an "ego desire." These are the desires of the mind, not of the soul.

Often, when we create a life that satisfies the people around us, we do it to protect the image of how others see us. In other words, our life matches our conditioned identity. When we are coming from this place of limitation, we focus on the results of our actions, rather than on the enjoyment of the process. For example, imagine a company executive whose colleagues envy her because of her status and monetary wealth. However, perhaps her dreams never had anything to do with where she is currently—maybe she wanted to run a Bed and Breakfast on a tropical island.

As you can see, real success isn't contained in the lists that others may have presented to us. Choosing to force a path that is not something your inner source resonates with is like swimming upstream, against the current. Sure, you can achieve what others think of as success, but it will never feel that way to the person who should feel it the most—*you*.

Ego desires will never stop coming up. As human beings, we'll always want to have something more than what we have. It is natural for us to have a thirst for the infinite. New desires will emerge out of nowhere and cross your mind every once in a while. That's okay. The main lesson here is that we should never find ourselves getting attached to ANY desire, regardless of whether it's coming from the physical-self, the ego-self, or the authentic-self. You will find that often, this desire will dissolve, but in the case that it does not, you will achieve it effortlessly, because it has become a part of who you are.

"A person who is not disturbed by the incessant flow of desires – that enter like rivers into the ocean, which is ever being filled but is always still –can alone achieve peace, and not the one who strives to satisfy such desires."
- Vyasa (from the Bhagavad Gita)

There is another critical thing I wish to point out. When your true life's path has been shown to you, dropping everything and latching on to that dream immediately can be a mistake. Of course, you'll see stories in which people have done this and succeeded. For example, more than one successful actor has left a small town to seek their fortune in a large city because they had an inner calling to be an entertainer. But when you look closely at their lives, their path was fraught with sacrifices and unpleasant circumstances. You can avoid going through many (but not all) of these challenges. Not only can some challenges cause unnecessary struggle, they can even stop you from achieving your dream, should they prove to be too much for you to handle. So, the lesson here is this: Take it slow if you must. Develop a flexible plan and surround yourself with people who will support your dream, either by giving you valuable advice or moral support. When you are surrounded with the energy of your desire, internal growth and manifestations can happen much faster.

There will never be an end to this journey. You are infinite in every way you can imagine. To say you *will become* your most authentic-self is a limited perspective. Shift to the frequency of always and constantly *becoming* your most authentic-self.

Exercise: Supporting your Soul's Longing

The following exercise will help bring clarity to what ignites your soul's longing:

1) Write down all the activities in your life that you do not love to do.
   - Job / career
   - Social activities
   - Daily practices

2) Scratch out the easy ones that you can stop doing immediately.
3) For the ones that are more difficult to stop doing:
   - Uncover the belief stopping you from dropping them (Follow the exercise in Chapter Two).

Look at these options from as many perspectives as you can, and record your thoughts. For example: "From the perspective of when I was younger…," "From the perspective of if there was a better opportunity available now…," "From the perspective of my desired future self…," etc. Once you view your situation from these different perspectives, it can be easier to recognize hidden blocks that may be stopping you from committing to change.

Now, begin brainstorming solutions to either outsource the "I Don't Love" activities on your list to others, replace them with activities that can get the same results, or drop them completely. When you do this, try to apply the principles outlined in this book. Remember, there is a path that resonates with your inner source and its intentions. Become mindful of the subtle changes you can be making and the opportunities you can be taking in your current life circumstances. Even the smallest shift can make a world of a difference.

Take note of the activities that bring you the most joy. Writing these down will do two things:

- It will help bring awareness to what these activities are, and
- It will turn these mere thoughts into objective truths. These may change overtime, so revisit this exercise whenever you feel called to (or every ninety days).

Observe what happens to your emotions and thoughts after you have participated in one or all these activities. Set up more opportunities to engage in these activities and *give yourself permission to enjoy yourself more often*. Look closely at how your daily experiences change ... but remember, do not expect an instantaneous response from the Universe (as per the 'Physical Reality Delay' mentioned in Chapter Three). Just take note of what is happening and how you feel throughout each day. Try not to become attached to anything—events, people, or emotions. Just be mindful of 'cause and effect.' Keep it simple. Even if you can't find the correlation between what you are doing and what reality presents to you, remember that there is something you can do: *Allow and trust.*

ALLOWING AND TRUSTING YOUR TRUTH

One of the main reasons people are held back with their manifestation process is that they do not trust their new perspectives—and often, this is because they do not see external confirmation of their new intentions. As we know, however, things are always moving, regardless of whether we can see them or not. To keep things moving in the unseen realm, we need to maintain conviction and faith that the desire will in fact manifest physically. The more conviction and faith we have, the more willing we will be to develop a new paradigm that gets us closer to what we want— even if that means stepping into the unknown.

I'm sure you have noticed that seeing yourself as someone who can create a life filled with health, wealth, love, and happiness can be challenging. You may ask, for example, "How can I feel like I'm wealthy when my bank account is empty?" Referring to your immediate reality can be a mistake. This is the reason so many of us feel stuck—and get stuck. We believe that it's easy when you're already wealthy to 'feel wealthy,' or that if we're already successful, it's easy to 'feel successful.' This is where many of us make a big mistake. For example, countless talented performers cannot see just how talented they really are. There are phenomenal singers who dread going on stage because someone important to them told them they weren't any good. There are also many people with great personalities and charisma who are unable to find love because of negative past relationship experiences. You and I know this to be true. This is what many of us do—we imagine that we are 'not good enough,' and we expect that we aren't going to get what we want. We deem our current life circumstances to be truth—and we get what we believe to be true. But what if we were to flip the script? Wouldn't a reality where you expect yourself to manifest the circumstances you desire be just as true? After all, reality is first created in the mind.

Once you understand this, you have accepted the existence of multiple realities. And if multiple realities exist, then it's safe to say that any perspective, no matter how absurd, can be deemed true. We create our reality through our perspective. Thus, all truths are true.

So, how do we measure this? Ask yourself these questions:

- Am I excited about who I am becoming?
- Do I truly want to be who I am becoming?
- Am I fulfilled about who I am becoming?

Asking yourself these questions redirects your focus back to what's important: your state of being and the direction you are taking your life. Once you realize what state of being you are in, you can evaluate better whether you are moving in the direction of becoming your future desired self. This is the only confirmation you need. Nothing external should replace this.

As we've talked about in a previous chapter, reality is always fluctuating. When the weather outside is gloomy, do you dwell on it? Or do you trust that it'll change tomorrow, or next week, or next month? Like the weather, life is always changing. We are never living in just one snapshot of reality. So, why focus on a temporary illusion? Why give perspectives that make you feel bad any attention, power, or energy? At this point, the only dependable vibrational reality is the one you are currently creating via your thoughts and emotions.

By consistently (there's that word again) placing your attention on moving forward toward your desired reality, you are, in essence, paving a pathway to a life that eventually will be confirmed physically. Just like the entertainer experiencing stage fright or the charismatic person who feels like they are unlovable, buying into a reality based on something you do not want is a waste of time. There are countless examples of this error all around us. You just need to recognize this—and act accordingly.

For some people, this might seem like a tall order. That's okay. Do not expect to jump right away from the vibrational frequency of a non-believer to that of a *knower*.

What you want to do is practice crystallizing new and empowering perspectives methodically—and consistently. Start with a perspective that is general and believable based on where you are currently, and then move up into more specific and ambitious ones. Notice yourself and your perspectives. Every time you perform an action, make a decision, or begin analyzing your circumstances, notice the perspective from which you are viewing your situation. Does it match the direction you want to be headed in? If so, continue standing in that place. If not, shift slowly into a place that does support where you want to go.

This practice is much like learning to play a musical instrument. A person should not expect to play their instrument at a concert level after a few weeks of practice. They start with basic chords and music theory, then they start playing jingles, then they move into playing full songs, and eventually, they compose their own music. As time moves forward, their expertise and creativity emerges as if it were a butterfly breaking free of a limiting cocoon.

If you wish to learn how to manifest with alignment, embodying your authentic-self consistently is key. Remember, you're overwriting a program you've been trained to follow your entire life. The good news is that it is easier than it sounds. That's because you will soon be motivated by seeing your desired results. Even the smallest confirmations, like finding a few dollars on the street, or getting complimented by a stranger, can serve as signs telling you "Keep going." At that point, it becomes easier to accelerate and stick to your vibration-altering practices, because you are slowly but surely trusting the process and allowing it to unfold.

UNCONSCIOUS SELF-DECEPTION

Embracing your authentic-self is not always easy. Oftentimes, we need to let go of many attachments, assumptions, and relationships we have in order to fully live through the values and ideals of our truth. During this process of change, we tend to defend the identity we've upheld our whole lives. The "you" that everyone knows you as. When this process starts, we fall into the pattern of lying to ourselves.

We tell ourselves we enjoy engaging in an activity, not because it's exciting or supportive of our dreams, but because it sustains our identity. For example, if John grew up with friends that enjoyed playing sports, he was more likely to take part in the same behaviors, actions, and activities. In other words, he was living through the same paradigm (a model of thoughts and behaviors) as his group of friends.

Now, as John grows up, he eventually realizes that he has a passion for playing music. However, whenever John separated some time in his schedule to learn and practice, he always received invites from his friends to play sports. To not disappoint anyone, or himself, he took up the invitation. This did not happen because he was being manipulated or peer pressured. Nor did it happen because he enjoys sports more than music. It happened because he needed to protect his sense of self and relationships. Without spending this time playing sports with the people he grew up with, he just wouldn't feel like "himself".

Now, deciding whether to spend time playing music or playing sports is not a massive deal. But what happens when we decide to take a different career path? Or develop feelings for someone that has different values than the ones we grew up with? To prevent conflict, we conform. To avoid discomfort, we hold on. When these patterns are repeated over and over again, we eventually start lying to ourselves, believing false truths to avoid facing the real ones.

Another angle we can take this is when we tell ourselves we will achieve something without ever taking the steps to achieve it. We say "I am going to manifest a billion dollars" but never sit down to read a book, study, and learn. We get too stuck in the non-physical realm of imagination and forget that we are living in a physical one as well. There is nothing wrong with visualization and future projections, but we must not forget the present moment. After all, it's the only moment that ever exist. Therefore, if we can't embody our vision in the here and now, we will only be sending out a signal but never receiving a response. We do not need to convince or prove to others that we are on the path to becoming who we want to be. We only need to convince ourselves, but only with truthfulness, and not with lies.

The key here to question your preferences and perceptions of the path you are taking. Do you truly enjoy what you do? Are those truly your dreams? Do you truly feel like you are embodying your desired future-self? When we are able to stop, reflect, and view our situation from multiple non-biased perspectives, we are able to see beyond the conditioning. The more we seek the truth, the easier it becomes to embody it and begin the process of honest and sustainable change.

THE DIFFERENCE BETWEEN FEAR AND MISALIGNMENT

One of the greatest obstacles we can face as human beings is the concept of "fear." Fear prevents us from achieving our goals, even when fear has no basis in our reality. When it comes to manifesting the things that will make us truly happy while also providing us with the material abundance we need in our daily lives, fear can stop us in our tracks. So, it's important to understand the nature of fear and how it's different from the idea of misalignment. In other words, we're going to break down the subtle differences between avoiding something because you fear it and avoiding something because it's not meant for you.

Being fearful is always associated with time. Fear can come directly from the memory of a past event that has either been experienced personally or that has been created in one's imagination. The potential effect that past or imagined events could have on a future situation is often the reason we avoid proceeding in a certain direction. For example, perhaps we are thinking of investing. We may have had an experience of having made a poor investment and losing money. Or we may have heard how someone we know was crippled financially after putting a lot of money into the same type of investment. We play out these events in our imagination, and when it's time to make the choice to invest, fear envelops us and we refuse to invest based on our experience, our current fearful thoughts, and our assumptions about future outcomes.

While this seems reasonable (especially for someone who does not have money to lose), there are other repercussions. What if, say, we put our fear aside and decide to study the ins-and-outs of this and other investment opportunities? Rather than making a decision based on the old state of being, we decide to make one based on deductive reasoning and with the intention of making the right decision, instead of avoiding making any decision at all. In other words, we move forward not by yielding to the old paradigm, but with the intention of building a new one. We become knowledgeable about our investment and make one that has potential for good returns, yet does not overwhelm us with fear of it not working out—a perfect balance. Even if it does not work out, the fact that we took a step forward with a new intention and a new state has already changed our vibrational reality to match a new paradigm. If it does not work out on this occasion, it will work out in the next one, or in the one after that. When you're able to tune into a state of complete conviction and knowingness, inevitably, reality will change to catch up.

"If it didn't open, it wasn't your door."
- Unknown

If your investment does work out, then it probably feels like the normal next step in your journey. It didn't just happen randomly. You changed how you saw yourself, and in turn, it changed your reality. This is what it means to change your vibration and frequency. We become determined to duplicate this feeling, so we wait for another opportunity to do so.

When making a decision based on an old state of being (tempered by fear), the reality created involved you investing without confidence, conviction, and allowing—and, most importantly, without faith. When you put fear aside and latch on to a new state of commitment, optimism, and the expectation of a new desired outcome (without getting attached), reality shifts in accordance with what would be expected from that particular vibrational frequency. In other words, you enter a reality compatible with the frequency of the emotion you felt when you decided to move forward with a new intention and state. It's a new way of being.

The fear of taking action is common—and so is the fear of loss. In all probability, this fear is one of the most controlling (and damaging) conditions possible. It has resulted in an untold number of missed opportunities, struggles, and other tragedies throughout the ages. The primary source of this particular fear has to do with our inherent need to feel secure. While this might seem admirable, it is in fact rooted in egoic thinking. For example, there was a time when human beings were more subject to harm if they encountered an unfamiliar environment. Many archaeologists would call this period "The Stone Age." Any sudden change in a person's surroundings served as a red flag—could danger be lurking around the corner? Therefore, in order to survive, our forbearers desired that everything remain the same.

That type of fear has become a part of our human biology, even for those who live in a relatively safe environment. Oddly enough, this type of fear tends to plague those who have found success in manifesting physical circumstances, such as wealth or a loving relationship. In some cases, it can become pathological, forcing a materially successful person to take extraordinary measures to secure their financial or relationship status. This is accompanied by a difficulty experiencing new things—and as a result, the successful person feels stuck or stagnant, and probably loses that which they initially found success in manifesting.

The fear of losing something is tied directly to believing in lack. This is precisely the reason this fear is based on illusion. This deeply rooted belief can be uncovered in the "Why?" exercise presented in Chapter Two. Since the Universe can contain everything except lack, any fear connected with lack is obviously a misguided perception.

For those attempting to learn manifestation, fear is often felt at a subconscious level. That's because we've been conditioned to believe that what is yours is not mine, and vice versa. We take ownership of our belongings as if they have something to do with who we truly are and what we truly want. Giving excess importance to material possessions will only create more unnecessary resistance.

In order to deal with this, you need to observe the benefits you are receiving by following the lessons in this book. As you are doing this, ask yourself periodically, "Why would I ever be afraid of letting go of attachment if it meant I could introduce more abundance into my life?"

On the other hand, decisions made to support your alignment, and to avoid misalignment, come from a state of knowing who you truly are and what you truly want. The reasoning involved is open-minded and not bounded by assumptions or limitations. In other words, you are moving with power rather than with force. When we limit the number of directions we can go in our lives, we limit the frequencies we can tune into. Often, we say to ourselves "I need to" or "I have to" do something to achieve a specific result. When we do this, we justify sacrificing our alignment. There are two ways to work around this. We can either reframe how we are viewing the path we are taking or have faith that it will take us to where we want to go.

It is important to note that although we are the creators of our reality, we do not create the spontaneous insights and creativity we tune into. We are merely vessels of expression receiving what is being channeled to and through us from the Universe. The reason this is important is because a new reality cannot be possible if it is coming from your current paradigm. If it's coming from your current paradigm, you will simply continue to experience what you are experiencing. Something new needs to be introduced: *inspiration*. Inspiration comes when we begin to see the world through a limitless lens. However, we can only tap into this unlimited creativity when we have faith that it exists in the first place. Trusting in the process, in your authentic-self, and in your ability to create your reality is essential to manifesting your dream life. When we see the world from a limited lens, the ideas that come are bounded and based on conditions. This leads to more misaligned actions and perspectives, and as result, misalignment.

A great example of taking misaligned actions is that of an employee who dwells on the idea that they need to please their supervisor constantly. If they do not, they think, they will not get a raise and will 'lack' money to pay for their dream home. While this is a different form of energy than the fear we discussed previously, it can also keep us from moving forward with our manifestation agenda. That supervisor is not in charge of all the money in the Universe. Fortunately, we can deal with this counter-productive behavior with ease.

First, understand that trying to override a vibrational frequency with an action is impossible. The act of *doing* will only produce the results you want if it comes from the right state of *being*. In other words, *actions can never replace vibration.* Therefore, just "working hard" or doing "hard work" will not cut it. Many people use action as a permission slip to tune into the vibrational frequency of their desire. This is why working hard on something you enjoy doing works, because it puts you in the right state of being. Hard work, on the other hand, can be counter-productive as it can require you to work on tasks that lead to moods and attitudes that go against the state you want to achieve.

Second, never feel like you *need* to achieve a specific result. Neediness will always build resistance toward the people and circumstances you want to attract. When we need something, we are telling ourselves vibrationally that we do not have it. Always focus on the *being* aspect of creation, and the *doing* and *having* parts will come in due time.

Identify the things you love to do—and do them often. At times, there will not be anything you are particularly passionate about, but there will still be opportunities for you to tune into this positive state (We will discuss more about this in the next chapter). When you act from a place of fear, you act from a state of stagnation, limitation, and worry. When you act from a place of love, growth, and potential, you act from a state that resonates with your desired reality. Remember, the authentic you is limitless.

CHAPTER FIVE

Presence Energy –
The Never-Changing Nature
of Your Being

O n a number of occasions, people have asked me, "When it comes to dealing with everyday life, how do you develop the correct mindset? How do you stay on track with your perspectives and intentions?" As we all know, life can distract us, and we can fall back into a reactive mindset easily. This chapter is about how we can conduct ourselves in our daily lives so it will be easier to stay positive, conscious, and in alignment with the creative energy of the Universe.

PRINCIPLE #5:
The Present Moment Is Always There.

STOP REACTING AND START RESPONDING

Life is like a mirror. When we smile at it, it returns the smile. If we give it an ugly look, it gives us an ugly look back. We're going to look at two distinct ways you can show up to your 'mirror of reality.' We'll do this by delving into the difference between responding to circumstances and reacting to them.

Think of a time in your life when you suffered from injustice. Maybe a coworker got a promotion you thought you deserved more, or a friend was invited to a social gathering and you weren't. If you weren't aware enough at the time, you may have reacted emotionally, and felt envious, disappointed, or frustrated. On the other hand, if you had reduced the importance you placed on such an event, you might have just carried on with your day, unaffected and peaceful.

It can be easy to fall into a victim frame of mind and claim that life is just unfair. But now that you understand more about the fabrics of reality, you know that when you react to reality, it reacts in kind. The longer you stay in a low vibrational attitude, the more momentum you build, and the more circumstances you attract that match your low vibration. Your initial choice—whether to respond or react—is the catalyst that sets the vibration in motion.

As we age, the tendency to react based on conditioned beliefs becomes a normal part of our paradigm. If, for example, those around you view a particular event in a negative light, you pick up on this perspective instantly. The more we allow ourselves to react unconsciously based on others' viewpoints, the more we become convinced that it's a normal part of life—that it's the right way to view the world. Giving away our power is "just the way things are." For most of us, it's the easy way out of taking responsibility for our state of being.

Our reactions are often unconscious behaviors rooted in fear. As we saw in the last chapter, fear can cause anger, frustration, hatred, sadness, or shame—and it's difficult to manage the conditioned thoughts and emotions that we have stored in our unconscious minds. However, what we can do is consciously intend to catch these reactions as soon as they happen. When we do this over a period of time, we build a trait called *resilience*.

A resilient person is one who recovers quickly from difficult situations. When we're able to do this, we stop negative momentum dead in its tracks. Being resilient gives us time to respond to any situation in a way that matches the attitude of our desired future self—we become adaptable, flexible, and open to the creative flow.

"It is not the strongest of the species that survives, nor the most intelligent that survives. It is the one that is most adaptable to change."
- Charles Darwin

When someone is adaptable, they are unattached to circumstances and outcomes. They are immersed in the events of life, but they are not moved out of balance by them. In other words, they set the intention to manifest a particular circumstance without falling victim to unmet expectations. They allow changes and challenges to come as they will, rather than forcing a specific path. This is called *redirecting* your reality.

This is different from being detached (which is essentially refusing to be a part of a given circumstance to begin with). When you are detached, you avoid experiencing unconscious reactions. If you never experience them, how will you know how to manage them? If you want to get better at the game, you need to play it as often as you can.

Note that we're not talking here about just 'surviving' the temptation to react to circumstances. We're talking about redirecting ourselves, about walking a path on which we can thrive, grow, and expand internally. We need to adopt a mindset that embraces difficult times rather than avoiding them. We need to learn to respond and to look at situations for what they are.

So, let's look back at our previous examples—the coworker who got the promotion you wanted and the friend who got invited to a social event you weren't asked to attend. Rather than contrasting what they got that you didn't get, and then falling back on a conditioned response such as bitterness (which is rooted in the ego-self), you could choose to respond with grace, compassion, and empathy. You could choose to be inspired by witnessing your coworker or friend winning—thereby opening yourself up to inspirations and insights. When you respond rather than react to situations, it's like you create a filter for your mind. You step into the role of observer / responder rather than thinker / reactor.

By practicing responding instead of reacting, you remove the power the ego-self and conditioning have over you. It's that simple. You'll be surprised how quickly this new mindset becomes a part of your go-to reactions in daily life. Notice I said "reactions" and not "responses"—because reactions *can* work for you, if you have practiced responding so effectively that your reactions empower you. After all, reactions can be negative, positive, or neutral. For most people, if they have unconsciously conditioned beliefs, given the ego's tendencies toward reacting negatively, their reactions will most likely be negative. While it is possible to have positive egoic reactions, staying open and aware is still the best mindset, because it allows you to be flexible, open, and receptive. After all, we never want to be a slave to our habits, reactions, or emotions.

We also do not want to adapt our goals or desires to fit our current circumstances or conditioned ego-self. We simply want to adapt our perception of reality to fit the narrative of our true goals and desires. Breaking down our desires into smaller chunks is a good way to build belief and practice responding rather than reacting. But remember: Never give up on a desire that is true to you. Be a thermostat in your life, not a thermometer. A thermometer reflects the temperature of its environment; a thermostat changes its environment to match its set temperature. Be the thermostat.

THE KEY TO MAINTAINING A HIGH VIBE

Adopting a mindset of responding rather than reacting has some great benefits—among them, becoming aware of how you relate to your surroundings. I'm sure you've heard (or read) a lot of advice that boils down to "maintain a positive attitude" or "a positive attitude yields positive results." While this is good advice, it's difficult for many people (after having spent their lives being conditioned to react negatively to certain events) to imagine looking at those same things in a positive light. A lot of people will just give up on positive thinking because their lives contain too many perceived negativities.

When you have made it a practice to respond rather than react to every situation that arises in your life, you will develop a mindset that will preclude you ever becoming a victim of your circumstances. Your new habit of responding opens your awareness to everything the Universe is showing you. For instance, when you are occupied with observing, intending, and allowing circumstances to happen in your life, there is no room for (and no need for) emotional reactions, or for fighting with or resisting unconscious behaviors.

We need to understand that we cannot control our reality. We can, however, create it. The reasoning here is that because our minds are limited, we can only come up with a limited number of paths, possibilities, and synchronicities before we run out of ideas about how things can or might turn out. On the other hand, the invisible field we live in is infinite. In other words, in this field of limitless potential, the paths, possibilities, and synchronicities are endless. It provides us with myriad probabilities and methods by which we can experience a manifestation—even ones without little to no resistance involved. Surrendering and having faith in your intentions is the most efficient way to manifest the life you want.

In order to adopt a higher vibrational way of living, despite the situations that might manifest on your journey, here is a technique called "The 3-5 Second Rule." Try it out!

Exercise: The 3-5 Second Rule

STEP 1:

When you first encounter a situation that you would normally react to, stop for approximately 3-5 seconds. Breathe.

If you end up reacting before you're able to catch yourself, that's okay. Acknowledge (internally, and to others around you if necessary) that you reacted unconsciously to the situation. Then repeat the first part of this step.

STEP 2:

As you are stopping yourself from reacting, be present. Make an intention in that moment to respond as the person you see yourself being in the future. Breathe.

STEP 3:

Acknowledge the reaction you would have as a result of this situation. Do not ignore it. If you ignore it, you are not engaged in changing your perspective. Only when you shine a light on your underlying baggage can you identify just where you will be making sustainable changes. Be aware that this baggage is no small thing. It consists of items that have evolved from various forms of conditioning: your past and present encounters, and your assumptions, prejudices, and beliefs.

STEP 4:

When the moment has passed, ask yourself: "Is this conditioned reaction I have to this circumstance helping me in any way?"

Should you decide that your conditioned reaction is not assisting you, ask yourself: "What response would allow me to continue my day in the most harmonious fashion?"

STEP 5:

See yourself as someone who would respond to circumstances based on the response you've given to the second question above. Embody this new intention—and never forget to breathe.

This exercise is not designed to change all of your circumstances and experiences in one go. Instead, it is designed to make you more aware of the small reactions you experience throughout your day that work against the state you want to achieve. Changing your state of being is not something you do just because it's the way to manifest your desires. It's something you do because it feels good. When you are in alignment with your true, desired vibrational nature, you are building a strong internal foundation so you can *then* begin to create and attract the external circumstances that match it.

BECOMING GREATER THAN HOW YOU THINK AND FEEL

Emotion is commonly defined as 'energy in motion.' So, naturally, when we hold on to, suppress, or repress emotions, we build resistance toward them. Before we can clear out our emotional baggage, we need to understand that holding on to any emotion blocks us from experiencing the healing process and the flow of creative energy. Allowing yourself to feel emotions and then letting them flow through you gives you a chance to transform your state of being.

This not only works with emotions, but with thoughts as well. Many people wrestle with negative thoughts by using other negative thoughts as a weapon, using it to strike out at flaws, point out weakness—and to judge, blame, and shame. That's not the answer, because when you resist something, you end up giving it more life. As the saying goes, *what you resist persists*. It's like fighting something while simultaneously giving it a hometown advantage.

I often mention, for example, that the reason working your way out of a harmful habit (such as addiction) can be so difficult is that you are working against your own mind. The subconscious mind you have built throughout your life sees through any 'tricks' you might conjure up and it in turn tricks you into doing things 'the old, tried-and-true way.'

One of the best ways to deal with thoughts and emotions is to shift into viewing them as separate entities. In other words, no longer identify with them. When you separate yourself from your thoughts and emotions, rather than having a conditioned (negative) perspective on something, you shift into a neutral perspective. Your thoughts and emotions are no longer 'my' thoughts and emotions; they are instead 'the' thoughts and emotions. Doing this removes the power your attention and engagement gives them. You are not your thoughts and emotions. You are something much greater. You are the master that controls the puppet. Do not allow the puppet to control the master.

> *"We can't solve problems by using the same kind of thinking we used when we created them."*
> **- Albert Einstein**

This is why one of the most important aspects of working toward mastering manifestation is to become aware of how your body and mind works. You will be amazed at how many times you react to a given situation in the same predictable manner. As you are dealing with conditioned reactions, it's likely you don't even realize it. More to the point, if your typical reactions were to be pointed out to you, you would likely try to justify or defend them. However, generally we don't have the time to analyze each and every reaction we have on a daily basis. Those who try to do this will soon get tired and go back to reacting to things the way they did in the past.

Therefore, when you are learning how to master your state of being, it's important to apply this technique: *View your thoughts and emotions from a neutral perspective.* You won't get the upper hand or stop them from appearing by holding them down and pummeling them into submission ... nor can you give them the control to run your life. You just give them room to happen, without engaging with them. This is a subtle practice, and it can take time to get used to. When you do this, you release any and all resistance—and when you stop resisting, all the intentions you've made to think better thoughts and feel better emotions will come to fruition. You are, in essence, giving yourself the opportunity to use your energy (that you might formerly have put into resisting a knee-jerk reaction) to do what needs to be done to embody more of your desired future self.

BODY PRESENCE

Presence can be found in everything, both living and nonliving. A pencil on a table, for example, has a certain presence, just like a dog or cat does. When we look deeply into any given moment of our experience, there is a sense of peace and quiet about everything, even when it may seem destructive and loud at first. Observing this layer of reality can awaken your senses and trigger instant present moment awareness. However, because of our five senses, it can be difficult at times to get all of them to focus on the presence of one object. For example, you could be trying to tune into the presence of a doorknob, but encounter difficulty in hearing the doorknob. Similarly, you can be present when a song is playing, but you can't reach out physically and touch the music. Therefore, one of the best practices for triggering present moment awareness is to tune into the presence of your body.

The benefit of using your body as an object of focus is that you are always feeling and sensing your body. It is never out of reach or distant from you. All of your senses are a part of this vehicle of experience. Essentially, you are using your senses to become aware of your senses. Often, we find ourselves lost in our thoughts or experiences, and as a result, we are not present in the moment. When our consciousness is too focused on our inner chatter or our outer experiences, we are not centered in our awareness. Being distracted, unconscious, or reactive is due to us not paying attention to where we are, what we are doing, and who we are being.

Next time you feel disconnected in the ways I've noted above, simply bring your consciousness back into your physical body. Notice the subtle sensations on your skin, the beating of your heart, the rhythm of your breath. This is an excellent tool for 'waking up' at any given moment throughout your day. The more you practice becoming present with your life experiences, the more conscious you are in your responses to them.

RESTING YOUR FOCUS

Our consciousness is the underlying source through which we receive, store, and recall information. Throughout our day-to-day lives, we find ourselves bombarded with content that resonates with fear, hatred, violence, and other forms of toxicity. Whether we are aware of it or not, this content is being fed to our consciousness constantly through our five senses. Everything we see, hear, touch, smell, and taste is registered and stored.

Therefore, if we're ever to find peace of mind and body, we need to stop consuming harmful content. Taking a moment to rest our focus in *nothingness* is one of the most profound and healthy things we can do to improve our state of being. Before we can begin to make real changes in how we are thinking and feeling, first we need to learn how to consume less and rest our focus more. Only then can we begin to build more awareness of and intention for the endless possibilities life has to offer.

I have already presented you with some principles and exercises to help you better manage your thoughts and emotions. While these are highly effective, I'm going to show you something else you can do—it's a fail-safe exercise that can cut through and reduce the intensity of most forms of overthinking and negative emotions.

What I'm about to tell you does not vary from person to person. There is one universal essence that remains constant within every one of us. You see, the same awareness with which you experienced life from birth to age five is the same awareness that experiences life at the age you are now. Life presents a wide variety of circumstances that can overwhelm our ability to perceive the truth about who we are. Think of a person swimming in the ocean who encounters weather conditions: for example, heavy rain, thunder, strong winds, powerful waves—all of which occur at the ocean's surface. That swimmer's way forward is controlled by the different conditions they experience on any given day. One day might be clear, sunny, and calm, so they enjoy the tranquil water while taking in a view that stretches to the horizon. On the next day, however, they might experience a violent storm with strong winds and waves they will need to overcome. While it may be simple to float on top of the water when the ocean is calm, will the swimmer be able to triumph over the huge swells that come crashing down on them during a vicious storm? Even if they are an extremely good swimmer, the answer is probably "no," and it might seem that their only option is to be tossed about at the whim of the storm.

While there are valid techniques that people can use to deal with such "storms," what about situations that can appear to be more than one can handle? We have the option to fall back on something that exists and never changes—the awareness that lies underneath our perception of daily events. That awareness can be compared to the depths of the ocean, which are never affected by the weather changes on the ocean's surface. You, as the swimmer, have the option to dive deep into those depths and take a break from the storms above.

All of us have this deeper awareness, and it is watching what we are experiencing (on the surface, so to speak) at any given point in time. It is the part of us that is observing the conditioned or unconditioned responses we have to life's daily circumstances. It is also the part of us that gives us the opportunity and power to shift our perceptions, to view things from new angles, and to reflect on how we perceive our circumstances. No other species on the planet has this ability to 'be aware of being aware.'

In essence, it is through *defocusing* that we can become mindful of how we perceive everything around us. Again, everything has a subtle presence, including us. When we're able to view the silence and beingness of the people, places, and things around us, we're able to tune into this presence energy. This time, we'll be tapping into the beingness of direct awareness. I like to call this practice "the awakening of 'I'."

The 'I' stands for the knower or observer behind experience. Its job is not to choose what is right, wrong, good, bad, true, or false. It's simply to observe reality for what it is and not for what label it should have. 'I' is neutral. When we take a moment to view our thoughts, our emotions, and our circumstances from I's neutral perspective, we give them space. We release resistance. We surrender.

This practice doesn't require much time, and is normally done during a meditation session, but it can also be done at any moment in the day. When we're hit with a wave of low vibrational thoughts and feelings, we can rest in a state of awareness that doesn't judge or label any experience. This is a way of detaching from the ego's view and shifting into the view of who we truly are.

For example, let's say you have a business that has just suffered a catastrophic loss and appears to be failing. Normally, you might become anxious about the outcome. Maybe you are angry about having to deal with it all. You might even become depressed when thinking about all the work you've done that suddenly looks like it was for nothing.

All these emotions occur on the surface of your perception. By shifting your awareness to that which lies below the surface, you connect with that deeper awareness. When you do this, the waves of low vibrational thoughts and emotions no longer become a part of your (ego-self) experience, but rather simply *an experience.* This will help with the dis-identification process that we've talked about before.

You could say that this is like pressing a reset button, since it gives you a chance to review and alter your perceptions of any given event or situation. At the least, it gives you a moment to stop the flood of resistance you would normally experience when encountering and fighting something that seems to be working against you. You can take a breath and remember that what you were about to experience was only one description of that event. As such, there is much more to that event than meets the eye!

This particular concept and exercise may appear more within the realm of philosophy than some of the other exercises I've covered. However, it's something you will want to consider, as it will offer you respite in every overwhelming situation. After applying this practice consistently, it will become more and more obvious why it's a waste of time to allow a seemingly negative circumstance to keep you from accessing your desired vibrational state. You will realize that you are much more than just the person experiencing it.

CHAPTER SIX

The Role of Your Thoughts – Bypassing the Negative Mind

I n this chapter, you will discover a truth that I have only alluded to until now. At this point, you have begun to realize the power we wield with our thoughts. Thoughts are the starting point through which every event in our lives takes place. Everything begins with an idea—and when we organize our ideas, we can understand who we are, what we want, and how to get it.

THOUGHTS GUIDE – EMOTIONS ATTRACT

One of the biggest Law of Attraction concepts many people misunderstand is that of "positive thinking." Have you ever been told that if you think positively, you'll manifest everything you want? Or that if you visualize yourself living your best life, it's bound to happen, eventually? Unfortunately (or fortunately), this is not the case. Because while positive thoughts help to build your vibrational frequency, they are not the only component of the manifestation process.

Our emotions play a huge role in our ability to manifest. They are the essence of our energy. In other words, they are like water to plants. Emotions move things into place. From a metaphysical viewpoint, emotions are creative catalysts we project into the infinite field, and they are how we relate to and connect with the world around us.

However, without thought, emotions are just scattered energy. Without a conscious guide, emotions would just run loose. Most people think unconsciously, and as a result, their emotions reflect this. Conditioned thoughts produce conditioned emotions, and when we put these two together, we create a conditioned state of being. This is why it can be so difficult to break free of the paradigm of poverty, illness, and struggle—especially if it's been conditioned within our family tree or social community.

In this chapter, I'm going to help you redefine your relationship with your thoughts. When you do this, you will have more control over the foundation from which your state of being is built. When we're able to better manage the never-ending flow of ideas that come through our subconscious minds, we can begin to reconstruct our inner reality. With consistent application and committed self-reflection, you will be able to turn your life around with an instant shift of perspective. It all starts when you understand this principle.

PRINCIPLE #6:
You Are Not Your Thoughts.

Each of us has the ability to guide our emotions. We do this with our thoughts. Think, for example, of a garden hose—and imagine that it represents your thoughts. Think of the water coming out of the hose as your emotions. Finally, think of the plants in the garden as your reality. For you to grow your plants (your reality), you will need to guide the water (your emotions) to them through the garden hose (your thoughts).

Thinking never stops. Since you are receiving signals, ideas, and content throughout your daily activities, it is wise to filter your thoughts. You can do this by choosing which thoughts you wish to resonate with emotionally. You do not have to resonate with every thought that passes through your mind. *You want to be an observer of thoughts, not a slave to them.* One technique you can use to assist you with this was mentioned in the "Resting Your Focus" section in Chapter Five.

> *"It is mental slavery to cling to things that have stopped serving their purpose in your life."*
> **- Chinonye J. Chidolue**

Rather than considering every thought that runs through your mind as "valid," step back. Watch your thoughts. When you give a conditioned thought the space simply to be, you create the space to facilitate its transformation. If you do this consistently, you (and those around you) will soon notice a change in your character. Instead of reacting to situations emotionally (and predictably), you will be more thoughtful and even-tempered. This is what it means to be *mindful.* This will prompt others to listen to what you have to say, since they can no longer assume what your response will be.

As a child, when I was around the grownups, I used to stay relatively quiet. I discovered that I could learn a lot more by listening than by talking. As a young man, I continued to sit silently in gatherings of friends and just listen. This had an interesting effect when I found myself in a group of friends who were engaged in a heated discussion. While everyone else was trying to make his or her point based on their emotions, I listened. By not giving in to my emotions, I had time to construct an informed response. Then, when I finally spoke up, everyone got quiet. Unlike what was going on in the discussion previously, no one tried to talk over me. Each person considered my words and gave them their full attention. You see, I had removed myself from their 'emotional pool' and chose the comments I wanted to project and the emotions I wanted to express carefully. We all have the opportunity to do this each and every single day.

My 'interruption' of the flow of conversation with my friends is similar to what happens when we 'interrupt' the flow of conditioned thoughts that come to our mind. When something unexpected occurs, everything comes to a stop and we can assess the new input. Therefore, it can be so beneficial to be aware of our 'normal' thinking habits and our reactions to everyday situations—and then to interrupt them. At that point, we are more open to accepting an alternative way of addressing a given situation. We go from having a negative thought process to having a neutral one due to the interruption, and finally, we move to a positive one based on our conscious choice. This can help us to make decisions that lead us to where we want to go—as opposed to making a decision that leads (once again) to the same old reality.

DISSOLVING NEGATIVE THOUGHT PROCESS

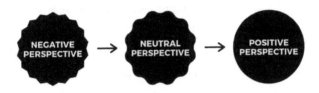

BYPASSING EXTERNAL TRIGGERS

Bringing awareness to thinking habits in this manner allows you to be limitless and infinite in your perspectives. The more you observe, the more non-attached you are to external circumstances. Giving yourself this power will allow you to be conscious of who you are being at any given moment in time. You will be able to choose your vibrational path.

I've mentioned on a number of occasions that consistency is the key to altering your thoughts and emotions to match your desired state of being. To do this, you must commit to no longer regarding external circumstances as cues prompting you as to how you should think and feel. This is a tall order. After all, you have been constructing conditioned reactions to your environment your entire life. It takes consistency and practice. Negative thoughts will dissipate once you are no longer feeding them with the energy of your attention and engagement.

Fortunately, this process has a snowball effect. Imagine a snowball rolling down a snow-covered hill. It starts off small, and increases in size dramatically the farther down the hill it rolls. Similarly, by following the teachings of this book, you will see some startling evidence that they really work. Once this begins to happen, you will want more and more, because you'll have proof and confirmation that it works. This will convince your subconscious mind to perform the suggested exercises consistently … if you do, you'll reap the rewards daily.

Exercise: Triggering the Observer

In this exercise, I give you a collection of moments you can use as prompts to remind you to shift into an observer role. In fact, this exercise can be bundled with many of the other exercises I have presented in this book.

Often, when we learn a new concept, it can be difficult to begin implementing it in our daily lives. It's as if we are trying to develop a new routine, except this routine is not happening physically (like making your bed every morning or exercising your body every day). Instead, this is a mental routine, and requires that you look past all the internal and external stimuli that can cause you to fall right back into your old patterns.

Here are some moments you can use as prompts to remind you throughout your day to shift into an observer role:

- When someone comes to speak to you (shift at the beginning of the conversation).
- When a new event happens around you (shift when the phone rings, when you hear a loud noise, or when someone appears, etc.).
- Before you act on something (shift when you are about to take a shower, go out for a drive, make coffee, etc.).

Remember, if you are taking thinking cues from your current situation unconsciously, it can be difficult to change the situation. If you are thinking and engaging with negative thoughts over and over again, won't this thinking pattern only serve to reinforce your reality? But when you reframe how you use your physical reality to pick and choose your thoughts and perspectives, your reality has no choice but to match them. That's because there is a direct correlation between what you see and feel and the vibrational reality that presents itself! When you change who you are, you will change what you do, and as a result, you will change what you have.

"All of our knowledge has its origin in our perception."
- Leonardo da Vinci

Practicing using your external environment consciously as a reminder of (and *not* as a reference to) how you should think and feel, is one way to help you crystallize more positive thinking patterns in your life. Another way is by having a North Star. A North Star is your "Why?" It's the main reason you want to change your life experience. The most powerful North Stars have to do with serving others—these others might be your family, your friends, or a community you feel compelled to serve. When we have a North Star, it serves as an anchor to keep us connected to our higher purpose. When we put out intentions from a place of purpose, mission, or contribution, we are more likely to stand behind them and be reminded of them.

It can be difficult to be inspired to change when your intentions are simply for material wealth, regardless of what that looks like. There is no problem with attaining material wealth—in fact, often, wealth is necessary so we can carry out our purpose. But again, if we're going to manifest from a place of truth, a North Star, connected to a higher purpose that is greater than you or me, will serve as a better tool for keeping you connected and focused.

THE EMPTINESS OF THOUGHTS

There are two main reasons our minds are filled constantly with chatter. The first has to do with our original development through evolution. The ability of human beings to multitask is an important step up from animals, for animals can only focus on one thing at a time. Animals are forced to "live in the 'now'"—they don't have the ability to go beyond their instincts and plan for the future.

Human beings, on the other hand, have always had the ability to multi-task mentally. For example, our forbearers, while thinking about where to go hunting next, might have been sharpening a spear. Perhaps it occurred to this same ancestor, at the same time, that they had forgotten to secure their cave against wild animals. Our forefathers became efficient at surviving by multi-tasking (and multi-thinking) effectively. But this built-in human skill no longer serves us, now that we no longer need to sharpen spears or worry about saber-toothed tigers stalking us in the night. In fact, this lack of focused attention is one of the biggest reasons why so many of us encounter difficulty in changing our reality. Lack of focus and scattered attention is a recipe for stagnation and slow progress. It's the equivalent of living an unconscious life.

The second reason our minds chatter is because we constantly define our environment and our reality. Our views are communicated to others, and we all reach an agreement—we all create and reinforce our views of reality and match those views to others' views of reality. This creates a group or societal paradigm, and all the individuals within this space have similar thoughts and emotions relative to a certain topic. Of course, there is always room for differences of perception, but not as much as you might think. If someone's 'mind chatter' creates a view of reality that is vastly different from the view of the majority's, that person can be deemed "delusional" or "crazy." On the other hand, they can also be labeled as a "genius" or "revolutionary." Remember, the ego-self does not like the unknown and it does not like change, so it does everything in its power to protect your current identity, so things remain consistent, stagnant—and limited.

In any case, the main point to consider is that our thoughts are not the sole reason for our manifestations. What if our realities were a direct manifestation of the chatter that runs through our minds all day? We would be living in chaos! Things would be manifesting all over the place, with nothing filtering the rate at which things manifested into physical reality. This is why we are designed to prioritize our manifestations through the filter of our emotions. Thoughts and words are *substance-less* unless we pair them up with emotions.

Adopting the new perspectives outlined in this book will not create the emotions needed for manifestation automatically, however. Why? Because your emotions will still emanate from your subconsciously conditioned belief systems. Beliefs are crystalized versions of perspectives. Therefore, to generate new emotions, you'll need to take time to live consistently through your new perspectives. When you begin to think new thoughts, take new actions, and say new words, new feelings will follow.

Your acceptance of new thoughts is tied directly to the emotions you're feeling at any given moment. So, for example, if you're feeling depressed, embracing blissful thoughts would be like climbing up a steep hill in a raging snowstorm. Therefore, the first step is to generalize your thoughts in order to generalize a feeling. Before you can do this, you need to know how to manage this constant internal chatter.

HOW TO END
OVER-THINKING FOR GOOD

While the most powerful tool in the realm of manifestation involves "non-thinking," this is a meditation technique that requires dedication and practice. However, we can get on the road toward manifesting our dream reality if we eliminate over-thinking first. We begin with a commitment to *stop judging*. Judging involves creating names, labels, and limited views that we apply to people, places, and things. When we do this, we form an attachment to these ideas.

Imagine that each idea we have is a dot in the sky. Our human nature is to connect the dots so we can make sense of them. We do this by creating stories. These stories fill the empty space between our thoughts. When we connect one train of thought to another and so on and so on … we are engaged in over-thinking. All it takes is one initial dot.

When we have no dots to connect, our stories can't exist. Without stories to fill the gaps between our thoughts, we can allow silence to exist in the gaps. That silence is what allows us to consciously connect with the infinite field—that place in the unseen Universe where infinite inspiration originates. This is another form of practicing mindfulness day to day. The more we empty our sky of labels and assumptions (dots), the more we actually see the truth of what is in front of us.

THREE PIVOTAL TECHNIQUES FOR ELEVATING YOUR STATE

Society limits us by prescribing which emotions we ought to feel when it comes to certain circumstances. But, of course, we have the ability to choose what feelings we wish to embrace in any given situation using our thoughts. You are capable of feeling any emotion right here, right now, regardless of what your external environment looks like.

"You can't wait until life isn't hard anymore before you decide to be happy."
- Nightbirde (Singer)

Emotions are the channels through which our soul communicates with us. If we feel bad or resistant, for example, it's because we are either choosing to believe in an idea that goes against our inner truth or we are unaware of underlying baggage. When we feel good and in flow, it's because our thoughts and emotions are aligned. When one or the other is off, we feel it.

Emotions are the voice of the soul—when we listen to them, we can begin the realignment process.

Exercise: Perspective Disruption

Here are three practices you can use to raise your vibration, realign your heart and mind, and dissolve negative perspectives effortlessly:

1) Practice creating a new humorous perspective about a seemingly negative situation, no matter how absurd it is. As Albert Einstein once said, "*Imagination is everything. It is the preview of life's coming attraction.*" Those who develop a strong imagination can be more fluid with their perception of reality. When we become conscious of how we use our imagination, we can change our reality seamlessly before our very eyes. When you feel like your perspective is out of alignment and is causing you to feel resistant to what is, flip the script. A powerful way to do this is to incorporate spontaneous humor into supposed negative situations in your life. Right before an event triggers a negative reaction from you, overwhelm the moment with love, humor, and positivity. This only needs to happen for a single moment to shift you back into a conscious, awake state.

2) Open your focus and broaden your view. When you do this, you give yourself the chance to view every 'negative moment' as an opportunity for growth and expansion. You can view any negative manifestation as a chance to learn and reflect and to become more conscious of your life's direction. When faced with something that might cause you to focus on specifics,

choose to expand your perspective. In other words, *always look at the bigger picture.* When you do this, you dissolve the excess importance you have given to the specifics. For example, say someone hits your car from behind when you are stopped at a traffic light. Your usual reaction might be to get out of your car and yell at the other driver. But the moment you step out of your car, you notice it's a nice day—the weather is pleasant, the sun is shining. So, you say, "Are you okay?" and you express relief that no one has been injured. Then you exchange insurance information and wish the other driver a safe journey to their destination. The car is not you. The situation is not you. You are much greater than any material thing or experience. Therefore, why expend energy unnecessarily? Instead, preserve it and use it to create and manifest the vision you have for your life.

3) Become more self-compassionate. It can be easy for us to blame ourselves for blaming others or get angry at ourselves for getting angry. This is a common pattern you can fall into when you are first learning about how to change your beliefs and perspectives. We have this tendency to kick ourselves when we are down. Not only does this trigger more reactions coming from that same state, but over the long run, it can turn into your default internal chatter. The best way to prevent this from happening, and to facilitate the process of change, is to be kind to yourself. Bring awareness to your shortcomings and work to improve them without judging yourself for having them. Be your most loyal fan. Even when you are down and low, be there for yourself and rise above it.

When we look at all three of these practices, we are addressing one big problem: Excess importance. In other words, we tend to care too much about what is going on in and around us. Assigning excess importance to internal or external circumstances is another reason we suffer. When the 'negative' conditions stay or the 'positive' ones go, we can feel as though we are either not enough or losing a part of ourselves. So, prompt yourself to replace the so-called 'normal' reactions you may have to life with a different response. Embrace your new perspective, rather than identifying with the fallback, old reaction you might have had before. By disrupting your perspectives, you allow yourself to see things for what they really are. You step (however briefly) out of the boxed-in, limited perception you might have had of the world.

Note that these practices are not *just* for learning how to cope with situations—we are transforming our environment. We are changing our vibrational attitude relative to the mirror of reality. Remember, the mirror won't smile back at us if we don't smile first.

Overcoming your conditioned perspectives is the first step. Once you've overcome them, your reality will look less like it's against you, and more like it's moving in your favor. When this happens, things will begin manifesting for you with ease and grace.

Practice creating a new perspective, one feeling at a time. As I mentioned before, change is facilitated through consistency and practice. However, it is also facilitated by addressing a situation one piece at a time. It is rare to find someone jumping from a low vibration to a high one instantaneously. However, when you shift into a positive perspective, you *do* instantaneously raise your vibration and shift closer and closer to the frequency of your desires. When you practice the techniques in this book and you see changes occurring in your reality, acknowledge your progress. Even when nothing changes, simply recognizing the new lens you've decided to see through is deserving of praise. When you can master your mind, you can master reality.

CHAPTER SEVEN

Emotional Empowerment –
Choosing to Let Go

In Zen Buddhism, the term *Shoshin* means "Beginner's Mind." The principal ideas behind this concept are that as we move through life's experience, we should remain open and assume nothing. Having preconceived notions or being attached to our ideas blocks us from maintaining a receptive state. For example, if someone sees themselves as an 'expert,' they are less likely to take in or even consider new information. In order for such a person to receive new information or experiences, they need to set aside their identity as an 'expert.' One cannot receive if they are not willing to let go.

Have you ever tried to hug someone when you're carrying luggage in both hands? It's quite difficult. Similarly, when it comes to life, many people carry baggage around, and when a new opportunity arrives, they can't embrace it. There is only so much we can carry with us before we block the infinite gifts life offers us—whether these gifts are opportunities, people, intuitive hunches, creative ideas—or even new positive perspectives and feelings. If we don't let go of our old thoughts and emotions, they will keep us from experiencing new ones.

In other words, if we constantly think the same thoughts and feel the same emotions, we attract the same kinds of circumstances into our lives. In order to change this, we need to be open to letting go of the old so we can embrace the new.

PRINCIPLE #7:
Let Go of the Old to Invite in the New.

INTELLIGENCE IS EVERYWHERE

One thing that should be apparent by now is that there is an intelligent force that exists beyond what we normally perceive. There are possibilities our limited minds can never imagine. This concept is called "Bounded Rationality." Human beings can only come up with a limited number of solutions to a problem before they run out of options. However, the invisible field that surrounds us is not bounded by the mind's rationality; it is infinite. Once we understand the limitlessness of our potential, we can (slowly but surely) begin to embrace it.

That being said, it is more efficient to put faith in a limitless source than to keep insisting on a limited one, wouldn't you say? Often, when someone has a positive manifesting experience, it's not exactly what they imagined—it's either something similar, or it's completely different. So, we need to remain open to letting go of the singular path we are on and allow ourselves to pivot when necessary—so we can recognize and embrace the other, better possibilities that can show up for us.

Once we begin to alter our state by using the principles and exercises in this book, we realize that we can no longer take things at face value. When I 'got' this, I was startled at how quickly I was manifesting, and how effortless and synchronistic life became. Things that on the surface looked negative had an underlying 'force' that propelled me toward a positive outcome. This happened because I was able to experience beyond my senses, think beyond my assumptions, and choose beyond my (supposed) limited options.

How does this work? Think, for example, of a person who is walking through a forest, happily enjoying the peace and calm. Suddenly, they trip over a root, fall down ... and rip their new pants. But as they pick themselves up, they notice a large gold nugget lying on the ground in front of them. If they hadn't tripped, they never would have seen the nugget. Instead of lamenting about their torn pants, now they have the means to purchase a whole new wardrobe!

When you begin to apply the principle of letting go, things like this will begin to happen to you (hopefully not the falling-down part!) at an ever-increasing rate. The only way it won't work is if you build up resistance to what you want. You see, reality manifests based on what you are resonating with vibrationally at any moment in time. Therefore, if you do not have faith that something is possible ... well ... it never will be, because it's not a possibility you are willing to consider or become aware of. If you identify with what is in front of you and believe that you need to move along a predetermined path in order to achieve success, your attitudes and limited belief systems will always create resistance towards what you want to manifest. But once you commit to trusting what lies beyond your current perception, you begin to trust the unknown. This is the first step in putting your faith in the Universe. When we surrender our limitations, we get into alignment with the unlimited.

SURRENDERING WHO YOU THINK YOU ARE

Negativity exists all around us. We see it in the news. We hear it on the radio. We watch it in entertainment and in social media. We work our way through our childhoods, being told what not to do and what cannot be done. Society does not tell us to "live our true nature" or "follow our excitement." Rather, we are told to "fit in" and "follow the course."

"They (children) learn that answers are more important than questions, and conforming is more important than originality and self-expression."
- Michael J. Gelb

Because of this, often we find ourselves on a path that doesn't resonate with what our hearts truly want. The longer we stay on this path, the more difficult it becomes to break free from conditioned thoughts and emotions. But here is where we need to assert ourselves. If someone says to you, "I demand that you feel sad and unhappy," what would your reply be? You would most certainly tell them that the way you feel is *your decision*.

Since this is the case, why would you not exercise that same *choice* when it comes to the way you perceive things? Once you understand that nothing in the Universe is ever set in stone, why give negativity any credence at all? Since all possible realities exist in the Universe, why choose to focus on the negative aspects that favor you least? Remember—you cannot change reality—you can only respond to it. That is what creates your reality.

In essence, by surrendering control over who you think you need to be, you give yourself permission to create your life experience based on your alignment—and nothing else. You must let go of who you unconsciously think you are and begin aligning consciously with who you *really* are. This is essential if you wish to welcome in a reality that is in alignment with your already abundant, joyful, limitless nature.

So, what does it mean to "let go?" Here is an exercise to help with just that.

Exercise: Surrendering to Infinity

To facilitate your empowerment, consider the following practices:

- Letting go of physical attachments –
  People hold on to material items, relationships, and jobs in the name of "tradition" or "security." The truth is it is easy to stay the same and complain about not experiencing change. This is because people have identified with what they have currently, and the idea of change threatens their current identity, or ego-self.

- Empty your cup of ideas to refill it with something better –
  Are you attached to beliefs, ideas, or ways of being? Are you filled with assumptions about how your life ought to be? If so, there could be an internal blockage that keeps you from accepting

new thoughts or adopting new perspectives. To change this, begin by adopting a Beginner's Mind, like mentioned in the beginning of this chapter. Only then will you be able to tune in to the infinite perspectives of our physical experience and begin changing your responses to it.

- Letting go of how you think others should perceive you –
One of the best examples of this can be seen on social media. There is nothing wrong with social media platforms, but when you are identified with who you appear to be, this can result in unnecessary anxiety and stress. Many people would rather focus on how others see them than focus on creating their own dream reality in 'real life.' The opinions of others can be similar to incoming negative thoughts. Remember: Observe them; do not engage with them.

- Letting go of other people's expectations –
Consider those who expect you to do and be what they think would be best for you. Often, these expectations come from those closest to you: family, friends, or partners. The fact is, only you can decide what is best for you. Nobody has all the answers. Listening to the insight, advice, and new perspectives that those you trust give you is a great way to get you thinking… but at the end of the day, your intuition will always ring true.

- Letting go of assumptions of how you think you need to act and be –
Within your subconscious there exists a wide range of conditioning that says, in essence: "In order to achieve XYZ, you must do ABC." Throughout our lives, we match these

expectations with our own hopes and dreams as we create our reality. A problem arises, however, when we build resistance to alignment and force ourselves to follow these arbitrary patterns. Working against the flow is equivalent to swimming upstream! Expand your perspective and new doors will begin to open up for you.

- Letting go of how you believe you need to feel and think –
  We all have conditioned responses that match the events that occur in our lives. When we allow ourselves to become a prisoner of these conditioned thoughts and feelings, however, we limit ourselves to a pre-determined 'script' for how we should respond to situations. When we commit to changing our reality, we also commit to changing these old mental and emotional scripts.

And, finally:

- Letting go of your attachment to what is –
  When you choose to change your life experience, everything changes. This includes the things you own as well as the relationships you have. Some will change a lot, some very little. As I mentioned earlier, if you fear change and try to hold on to the familiar, things remain the same. Mastering the Laws of Manifestation implies that you have the ability to enact change. Rather than tightening your grip on what exists currently, allow change to happen!

The essence of letting go is moving beyond the narrow, single path of your current existence and opening yourself up to an infinite number of new pathways. In order to attract the things you truly want in your life, you must be ready to feel and act according to those desires. This new form of attraction entails both letting go of your resistance to change and making peace with everything in your life. When you're ready to say, "I understand how things are and I accept it, however, I intend to change it," you will be open to allowing new things to manifest in your life.

"Change happens when the pain of staying the same is greater than the pain of change."
- Tony Robbins

As you can see, ironically, to be empowered is to surrender. I'm not referring to the type of surrender that involves waving a white flag and giving up on your desires. The type of surrender I am speaking of involves releasing the resistance that stops you from obtaining your desires.

Surrendering involves being at peace with what is. *This peace must come from the knowledge that where you are at currently is the beginning of the journey to where you want to go.* The mistake many people make is that they push against the things they feel they don't want. They do this in a couple of ways. For example, some people feel they have lost something—and they are fearful of losing even more. But, by comparing what they once had to what they have now, they are merely holding on to the past and resisting the present. This is not 'letting go.'

Another mistake people make is comparing what they have now to what they want for their future. This is also not 'letting go.' As long as we view our current situation from a negative perspective, we will continue to attract circumstances that match it. When we embrace our current situation, knowing that it is a starting point on a new journey, we allow the Universe to assist us in manifesting our desires. Rather than intending to improve our manifestation abilities, we ought instead to let go of what holds us back and choose to receive new experiences.

Exercise: The Letting Go Process

The letting go process can be broken down into three steps:

1) Acknowledging:

   Refusing to acknowledge your current circumstances is simply a form of ignoring the reality you wish to change. Change cannot occur unless there is a starting point. How can you intend to manifest a better situation if you refuse to acknowledge the one you are currently in? In a way, this is a form of self-delusion led by the ego-self. The ego-self defines its existence and its worth based on what it is experiencing physically. Thus, if circumstances are not ideal, it will look for reasons as to why. This is when we blame others and play the victim. This holds true for every aspect and area of life.

   As such, when feelings of sadness, guilt, anger, frustration, victimization, etc. are present, we need to acknowledge them. Trying to escape from your feelings will only suppress them—and when we suppress our feelings long enough, they begin to control our lives from within the unconscious parts of our minds and bodies.

2) Accepting:

The second stage of letting go is to accept this truth: You are a human being and human beings have emotions. There is no reason to view your emotions in a way that disempowers you. Feeling guilty, ashamed, or frustrated about how you feel are just a few examples of emotions that can disempower us.

Problems arise when we attach ourselves to negative emotions and allow them to define our experiences. When we feel sad, for example, it's common to create the story that we are sad people. But when we define ourselves in this way, ultimately we are 'boxing in' what is and creating resistance around it. What if, within the negative experience, there is a lesson to be learned? Wouldn't learning the lesson make the experience more valuable? Of course it would. This is how the Universe works—it is always in the process of creating disorder, chaos, and ultimately, change. Change is normal. Discomfort and chaos lead to growth and novelty. This is what manifesting is all about.

The bottom line? You need to give yourself permission to feel however you are feeling, without judging yourself or your emotions. The more order you try to place upon a given process, the more resistance you build. Allow your emotions to exist, because whatever you are feeling is shining a light on your unconscious perspectives and beliefs. View your emotions as beacons, and you will no longer feel the need to run away or allow your feelings to hold you back.

3) Making the Choice:

The final stage of letting go is making the choice to do it. You must *choose* to let go of your past conditioned emotions. Old emotions are anchors that keep you stuck in an old identity. When you make this choice, you refuse to feed the ego-self. You must make this intention, because by doing so, in effect, you choose to let go of everything in your life that correlates with these old emotions.

Now, the way to make this choice is by dis-identifying with the emotion you wish to let go of. When we dis-identify, we disown, and that which we do not own can't have any effect on us. This is how we create the internal space needed for change.

The next part of this step is to question your emotions. When you ask yourself questions, you become conscious of your unconscious, thereby bringing pent-up emotions up to the surface. Every person is different and will get results within a different time frame, depending on the intensity and quantity of their suppressed emotions. However, we can all start by asking four simple questions:

a. Am I willing to allow this emotion to come up?

b. Am I willing to feel into this emotion fully, without judgment?

c. Am I willing to let go of this emotion?

d. When am I willing to let go of this emotion?

Once you have committed to letting go of emotions that no longer serve you, you are also letting go of people, places, and things that keep you out of alignment. These can come in the form of an abusive relationship, a negative social circle, expectations of others, or fear of failure. So, you might ask yourself: "How will I know when I have finally let go?" You can lay this question to rest by asking yourself these final two questions:

a. Am I okay with letting go of the people, places, and things that keep me out of alignment?

b. Am I okay with not manifesting my desire in the way that I expect to?

By asking (and answering) these questions, you will be able to determine whether you are still attached to your current circumstances, desires, and expectations. This is also an excellent litmus test that will tell you if you're truly embodying the version of you that resonates with your desired reality. Remember, before we can have, we must *do* … but before we can *do*, we must *be*.

If you answered "yes" to both of these questions, you are well on your way to increasing your receptivity and activating the 'receiving mode.' This is the mode in which you are open to manifesting new and unknown creations and experiences.

Choosing to be (and being) proficient at letting go is an excellent way to recalibrate your frequency and alter your path toward your greater goals. Lingering and dwelling on the past brings stagnant energy, and stagnant energy keeps you feeling stuck and resistant toward what you truly want.

If you answered "no" to either of these two final questions, you need to uncover the hidden beliefs and perspectives that hold you back. Fortunately, by following the suggestions I have outlined in this book, that task should not be difficult. After you have identified the issue, you're free to work on letting it go and manifesting from a place of freedom rather than from a place of limitation.

Conclusion

"You can't have a satisfying ending with an unsatisfying journey."
- Abraham Hicks

Now that I have presented you with the Seven Hidden Principles that will keep you mindful and in control of your thoughts and emotions (so that you can manifest with ease), I want to point out a few things. First of all, manifestation is far more than just 'wishing' for change or writing a list of all the things that you want to have happen in your life. It also requires far more than reading a few books, attending a few seminars, or applying a few techniques. Although books, seminars, and techniques can be helpful and can lead you to a better understanding of yourself, they will not solve all your problems. You need to do the deep self-reflection and the transformational inner work.

Your outer world is a reflection of your inner world. How you see yourself, your situation, and your potential is exactly what your reality reflects back to you. So, when you're able to understand the principles in this book, apply them, and *live by them*, then the techniques you use naturally increase in effectiveness, and as a result, your desired manifestations really begin to take form.

Once you understand that manifestation is something you

already do continuously, you will know that the goal is not about the 'act' of manifesting. It's about tuning into the reality you want to experience by shifting into the proper energetic frequency. This task involves making several changes in your way of thinking—from the conscious to the subconscious and unconscious levels. It involves gaining clarity about what you truly want and who you truly are. Once you have a North Star, you can begin to apply the extremely important lesson of "responding instead of reacting." Awareness of your behavior will help you identify the hidden, conditioned reactions that have kept you running on autopilot. Learning to let go of the things and concepts you have been clutching your entire life will allow you to open up to new perspectives and experiences.

In this book, I have given you tools to help you end the cycle of allowing your conditioning to define your reality. I have done this in a way that will help you understand that leaving your old self behind is not a loss—it is the start of a new journey. This new journey involves releasing the heaviness of attachments that keep you stuck on an unfulfilling path. In this way, you can begin your new journey with an internal lightness that paves the path to a more fluid, flexible, and adaptable lifestyle.

There is a saying that goes like this: "*Most people overestimate what they can do in a day or a week, but underestimate what they can do in a month or a year.*"

Progress is progress, no matter how small. Use your little moments of progress as confirmation that you are moving toward where you want to be vibrationally. Eventually, momentum will pick up.

These practices should not be applied only through effort, however. They also require intention and allowing. The difference is that *effort* focuses on physical force, while *intention* and *allowing* focus on vibrational power. Effort is the opposite of allowing. Therefore, when we put effort into practice, we're not allowing ourselves to fully embrace the benefits of this practice. We're closing ourselves off to its potential.

The only way effort can be beneficial is when you are redirecting your actions—in other words, when you are shifting your intentions. Think of it as sailing … your effort should be used to move the rudder (to redirect the boat's course). What is actually moving the boat (your reality) is the position of the sails (your intentions) relative to the wind (the flow of life).

The Universe doesn't need you to prove anything. It needs you to *be* it. Set your intention, take actions that support your dreams, and go to sleep knowing you did enough. At the end of the day, this is all it takes to manifest the life you want with ease. Back up your intentions. Stay in alignment. Avoid or reframe anything that makes your life feel overwhelming or draining. Stay in balance—reduce the importance you give to your inner and outer reality. Be greater than all of it. Take action to get what you desire, but allow it to come to fruition naturally. Don't force anything. And most importantly, have faith. Only then will you reap the true benefits of and creativity from your actions.

The power required to live a life of abundance, love, and freedom is *within you*. You no longer need to be concerned about following pre-paved paths or ideologies. This is because your path will be laid out before you, whether in the form of a challenge or blessing—and that is as it should be. The subtle shifts and turns you need to take will be clear once you've cleaned your lens of perception and understood how to play with the instrument of your mind and body.

I'm truly grateful to have had this opportunity to help you prepare yourself for a life defined by true alignment. Now it's up to YOU. You have the tools—don't procrastinate. Make the changes. Reap the benefits. Above all, enjoy the journey!

A Short Message
From The Author

Hey there, did you enjoy the book? Hopefully you did! A lot of work, research, and collaborations took place to make this book what it is today. So if you enjoyed *Manifesting With Alignment*, I'd love to hear your thoughts in the review section on Amazon.com. It helps me gain valuable feedback to produce the highest quality content for all of my beautiful readers. Even just a short 1-2 sentence review would mean the WORLD to me.

>> Scan the QR Code below with your smartphone
to leave a short review on Amazon <<

Thank you from the bottom of my heart for purchasing and reading it to end.

Sincerely,

Rynn

REFERENCES

Albigen.com. (n.d.). *The most rapid means to eternal bliss. The awareness watching awareness practice instructions.* https://albigen. com/uarelove/awa_instructions.htm

Anka, D. (n. d.). *Some of the core concepts of Bashar from the Essassani civilization.* https://iasos.com/metaphys/bashar/#challenge

Clear, J. (n. d.). *Why facts don't change our minds.* James Clear. https://jamesclear.com/why-facts-dont-change-minds

Dispenza, J. (2018, August 17). *Accessing the infinite database.* Dr. Joe Dispenza. https://blog.drjoedispenza.com/blog/ consciousness/accessing-the-infinite-database

Freud, S. (2001). *Complete Psychological Works of Sigmund Freud: The Interpretation of Dreams* (Vol. 4). Random House.

Gone Viral Entertainment. (2021, June 9). *Nightbirde – Woman fighting cancer gets Simon's golden buzzer – America's Got Talent – 2021!!* [Video]. YouTube. https://www.youtube.com/ watch?v=bTJ3eeYrHI4

Gelb, J. Michael (2021, April 28) 7 Leonardo Da Vinci Exercises to Awaken Your Genius. Mindvalley. *https://podcast.mindvalley. com/tag/michael-j-gelb/*

Mosmuller, M. (2017, August 23). *The substance of thinking.* Mieke Mosmullers Philosophical Reflections Blog. https://www. miekemosmuller.com/en/blog/the-substance-of-thinking

Puiman, R. (2015, December 2). *Your gut feeling: Fear or intuition.* Huffpost. https://www.huffpost.com/entry/your-gut-feeling-fear-or-_b_6667194

Quazi Johir. (2020, December 3). *How to master your emotions: The 4 step "release" process that changed my life* [Video]. YouTube. https://www.youtube.com/c&list=PLwryVAXS0c4Gsp3coYkNS LHU0VTVZgsKS&index=6

Spiritual Awakening Process. (n.d.). *The fear of the unknown.* James Tolles. https://www.spiritualawakeningprocess.com/2017/03/ the-fear-of-unknown.html

Made in the USA
Las Vegas, NV
19 August 2021